Life, the Universe and Everything

Life, the Universe and Everything

42 Meditations for Lent and Beyond

David Wilkinson

British Library Cataloguing in Publication data

A catalogue record for this book is available
from the British Library

ISBN 1-85852-321-4
978-1-85852-321-7

First published by Inspire
4 John Wesley Road
Werrington
Peterborough PE4 6ZP

Printed and bound in Great Britain by
Stanley L Hunt (Printers) Ltd, Northants

Contents

Introduction

In Douglas Adams' classic *The Hitchhiker's Guide to the Galaxy*, a computer, Deep Thought, is constructed to answer the question to life, the universe and everything. It comes back after many generations with the answer '42'. At this point, of course, another computer has to be constructed to find the question! There is a real sense in which the questions are as important as the answers.

Pop culture today is full of questions. While some in the Church want to condemn *The Da Vinci Code,* millions have read the book and seen the movie. Whatever you make of its artistic merits, it poses some fascinating questions about the man Jesus and the history of what people believe about him. Television series such as *The Simpsons* and *Desperate Housewives* explore questions of love and the meaning of life with irreverent comedy. Life in a media-dominated culture continually poses the question of what it means to be human, whether it be through Robbie Williams or U2 on my iPod, the adverts asking me to change my clothes, hairstyle and toothpaste or in the reality television of *Big Brother.*

Too often, Christians have ignored or demonized pop culture, such as television, movies or popular music. It has been characterized as either 'trivial entertainment' or the work of the devil and, therefore, Christians should stay well away for fear of contamination. The Harry Potter books have thus been condemned as leading children into the occult, Hollywood has been criticized for its lack of sexual morality and television soaps have been written off as mindless pulp. In such a climate, a similar attitude has been voiced regarding sport, science and technology, saying that they are either threats to the gospel or providers of false salvation.

This book takes a different view. It assembles 42 observations of contemporary culture to provide a way in to reading passages from Luke's Gospel. It takes the questions posed by pop culture seriously, as a way to gain insight into Christian faith. Why should such everyday things be in a fruitful dialogue with the Bible? Christians would see this as being because the God of his written word is also the God of creation – a creation that has Jesus as Lord and where the Holy Spirit is continually at work. We would therefore expect that the Bible can help us to understand certain aspects of pop culture, and pop culture can help us to understand certain aspects of the Bible, not just in terms of illustrations, but in the posing of questions to one another.

Yet, this is not a book that explores such questions at a philosophical level and in a philosophical style. Rather, it is a series of case studies, the purpose of which is to lead you into a deeper relationship with God. Therefore, you will find in the structure of this book considerable space for you to explore the dialogue between popular culture and the Bible. Rather than the observations from contemporary culture coming after the Bible passages and being used to explain these passages, the order is reversed. We look first at popular culture and then try to find resonances, challenges and opportunities in it for the Christian gospel. For those of you who are beginning to explore the Christian faith, this may be enough. However, for others who want to explore further, there are suggested Bible passages from the life of Jesus, further questions to think about and prayers that offer possible ways forward. The questions posed are worth pondering in this process. They are open-ended to give you space to think about and examine your own life. Some of you might want to have them in the back of your mind as you travel to work or do the shopping. Some might find it helpful to note down a few responses in a notebook. Not all of the questions will call for the same kinds of responses and so, while reading this book, you may want to concentrate on a few questions rather than all of them.

Of course there are dangers in popular culture. Some of it does have harmful content – not least the way it can subtly squeeze individuals and cultures into a mould of consumerism, thus devaluing other human beings who do not have fame, fortune or bling. These tendencies must be resisted and critiqued, but this can be done more effectively by those who understand popular culture rather than those who shout out blindly from the touchline.

Throughout Luke's Gospel there is a theme that keeps reappearing. Jesus eats and drinks with tax-collectors and 'sinners' and is criticized for it (Luke 5.29–30; Luke 15.1–2; Luke 19.7). Here is Jesus, at the centre of his culture, enjoying it and at the same time offering the good news of salvation. I long to see the day when Christians will approach our culture in the same way.

This book has arisen from a number of 'Pause for Thoughts' given on BBC Radio 2 and it is a pleasure to thank the different producers who have worked with me over the years and helped me to express myself in clearer ways. I am also thankful to the Methodist Church and St John's College, Durham, who have supported me financially in this ministry of attempting to speak of Jesus in contemporary culture. Ideas, of course, have come from many and various conversations, but, in particular, my wife, Alison, and my children, Adam and Hannah, have been great companions in enjoying, understanding and seeing God in popular culture.

David Wilkinson
St John's College
University of Durham

Day 1

Eating more chocolate for Lent?

The beginning of Lent last year had an odd feel about it. The period of time when Christians traditionally give up chocolate saw me doing a rather unusual thing. I was at a science museum and it had a special exhibition on the science of chocolate. Of course, one cannot do strict scientific experiments on chocolate without tasting it and so there was free chocolate in abundance!

One of the experiments was to see the effect of chocolate on memory and mood. We were set tasks then given chocolate and asked to repeat similar tests. 'Binary Bill', a mad scientist, then informed us of the facts about different types of chocolate, its benefits and its dangers and, of course, offered us more chocolate to sample these differences. Finally, we were given marshmallows to dip into a chocolate fountain, which, I am sure, will be on every street corner in heaven.

What is our fascination with chocolate? Many of us will identify with the mantra, 'When the going gets tough, I need more chocolate!' Why, then, is chocolate a popular thing to link with Lent? Lasse Hallström's movie *Chocolat*, based on the novel by Joanne Harris, tells a story that, despite its Hollywood sentimentality, raises a number of questions about how Christians look at the world. A travelling single mother opens a chocolaterie in an outwardly religious French village during Lent. The mayor sees himself as the religious guardian of the village (indeed, in the book, the mayor is also the priest). While publicly labelled as sinful, chocolate becomes a medium for healing and redemption. It is a movie that asks questions about how religion can sometimes devalue the gifts of this world.

Lent is a time when we ask the question, 'Are the attractive things in the world temptations to be avoided?' Some can certainly become idols that dominate our lives and give us a sense of security away from God. While we might joke and do mad-science experiments on chocolate, more serious idols – such as money, power, fame and technology – can give us a sense of independence and invulnerability without God. Equally, religion can also become an idol and then give a false sense of salvation. We think that God will love us more if we sacrifice things for him. We think also that if we say our prayers regularly, then God's arm will be twisted to give us an easy life, full of health and wealth.

Lent is a time to see what our idols are and to break our reliance on them. It is not an excuse to reject God's good gifts of creation in order to endear ourselves to him. So, why not take something up for Lent? Read this book daily and set aside a little time to read the Bible and say some prayers. There is no guarantee that it will make you feel better in the short term – for that, you will need copious amounts of chocolate – but, in the long term, it will be a much more sustainable diet.

Bible reading
Luke 4.1–13

Something to think about
In what areas do I fall into temptation?

Prayer
Lord Jesus, you know what it is like to live in this world surrounded by the gifts and joys of creation, and surrounded by temptations. Help me to live faithfully, resisting evil and enjoying fully the good. Give me grace to discern between them. Amen

Day 2

Harry Potter: hope for the end

I came late to Harry Potter. My wife and son had read *Harry Potter and the Half-Blood Prince* within the first week of its publication. It took me a few more days, during which time they were banned from discussing the twists of the plot.

In fact, they were way ahead of me in terms of the first five books. I stayed clear of Harry Potter until a number of long family car journeys were redeemed by Stephen Fry reading the books on CD.

Now, I cannot wait for the next book. I want to know whether the Half-Blood Prince really is lost to the dark side. Will Hermione and Ron get married and have a family of know-it-alls with ginger hair? Most of all, will Harry survive his inevitable encounter with Voldemort?

J.K. Rowling tells a good story. While I love the characterizations and humour, mainly I am gripped by the story in its movement towards its resolution. For, in the anticipation of the end and intrigue of how that end will come, the story is given meaning and purpose. That's why the final book is so important. The end is often the key to the whole thing.

The end is also key to the Christian story. In the Bible, God's relationship with human beings is told in terms of a story. Genesis gives the beginning and context to this story in the creative acts of God. Not unlike some elements of the Harry Potter story, the biblical story tells of the battle between good and evil, the importance of choices and the possibility of human transformation through love.

What about the end? Here is a major difference. The Christian faith holds that the inevitable battle between good and evil has already happened when, in the cross and resurrection of Jesus, we see that love conquers evil, sin and death. This is more than a clue to how things might turn out. It gives me, as a Christian, not knowledge of everything in the future, but the assurance that, ultimately, good *will* triumph.

So, I ask myself, 'Why do I believe that the Order of the Phoenix will triumph over the Deatheaters? Why do I hope that there is redemption for the Half-Blood Prince?' Partly it is my attachment to the story, but also it is partly because, despite many experiences in this world, I believe that, in Jesus, I see that good is stronger than evil.

Bible passage
Luke 4.14–30

Something to think about
If I believe that good will triumph at the end, how does that affect how I live my life today?

Prayer
Lord of the past and Lord of the future, be Lord of my present. May I live in the light of the future hope that you give. Give me confidence to do the right thing with the knowledge that nothing I do for you is in vain. Amen

Day 3

The search for a superhero

Clark Kent is back yet again. Not content with his early years in *Smallville,* Dean Cain's television portrayal or Christopher Reeve's movies, which convinced some of us that a man *could* fly, *Superman Returns* is now back on the big screen. He is joined by *XMen 3* and earlier blockbusters such as *Spiderman 2* and *The Fantastic Four.* I love these movies for their special effects and escapist adventure, but I cannot fail also to see some deeper questions.

Why is the superhero genre so popular? It does seem to tap into our sense of needing a redeemer – someone greater than ourselves who will deliver us from the mess that we have got ourselves into. Yet, such superheroes triumph through self-sacrifice.

A book by two American academics suggests that the superhero story has grown specifically because of the Christian foundations of our culture. Now, that's not to say that Jesus drove a Batmobile and Peter should really have been called Robin. What it is saying is that the belief in someone who is greater than we are, yet like us, who comes to save us, has been embedded in our culture because of Christianity. Indeed, the trailers for the *Superman* movie use explicit biblical concepts and language to talk of a special son sent to the Earth to save it.

My own faith as a Christian is exactly about a hero who comes to save me. That hero lived a long time ago and defeated evil not through clever technology or genetic enhancement, but by the power of self-giving love. I may not have to face Lex Luthor on a day-to-day basis, but there are times when I acknowledge my need of help. How can I live the kind of life that God wants me to live and the kind of life that I know makes me fully human, resisting evil, caring for strangers and defeating sin? In all of this, I find that Jesus is my deliverer and helper. Indeed, that route of deliverance is achieved by his self-giving love on the cross.

I am called to follow that pattern of self-giving love, reliant on his companionship and power. I suppose I am called to be a side-kick. In fact, come to think of it, that's the Bible means by a disciple. I'm just thankful that Jesus' disciples do not need to wear their underpants over a pair of tights.

Bible passage
Luke 4.31–44

Something to think about
Are there areas of my life where I need help?

Prayer
Lord, you are my hero – someone I can look up to. Lord, you are also my friend – ready to help. Lord, you are the defender of the weak and the alienated, wanting me to follow you. Holy Spirit, give me the power that I need to live the Jesus life. Amen

Day 4

Football managers, *The Apprentice* and the leader

What makes a great leader? Debate within both psychology and business studies has revolved around whether masculine or feminine characteristics are the most important. Programmes such as Alan Sugar's *The Apprentice* or the American version with Donald Trump pose such questions. Is the traditionally male tendency to lean towards aggressive competitiveness more effective in getting the job done than the female skills of networking and empathy?

Football managers are certain kinds of leaders, and few would demonstrate being in touch with their 'feminine side'! Indeed, for some of them, the closest they get is in the 'hairdryer' treatment meted out to badly performing players. Other managers are expert at teacup throwing or the flying boot method of inspiration. The late Brian Clough once encouraged one of his stars after his international debut by saying, 'Son, you are the first person to play two games for England on the same day.' When the player looked puzzled, Clough went on, 'Your first and your last.'

Even if such tactics do not work, football managers can always get rid of troublesome or badly performing players in the summer transfer window, but should leaders stamp their authority in such a way?

In a completely different context, I saw a young business executive the other day with a T-shirt on which were the words, 'Jump over the injured, ignore the dead, don't waste time on the weak'. I bet his was a happy company to work for.

One of the extraordinary things about Jesus of Nazareth is that he gave a completely different model of leadership. His team of 12 disciples included weak, impulsive and confused outcasts and one who would betray him in the end. Indeed, the New Testament is tabloid-like, pointing out just how stupid and unspiritual they were. Yet Jesus believed in them, loved them and knew that the love of God could transform them. He used them to revolutionize the world. In that he was right, and over one billion people in the world are Christians because of them. As a Christian, the God I see in Jesus is not a boss who casts me aside when I make a mistake, but someone who offers me forgiveness and help.

Interestingly enough, some secular leadership models are beginning to move closer to these ideals. They talk not about the imposition of authority but, rather, the emergence of authority through example, respect and transformation.

The test of a great leader is not just the ability to make difficult decisions but also the ability to mould a team from a group of difficult people.

Bible passage
Luke 5.1–11

Something to think about
If I am to be a leader or part of a team, how should I work with difficult people?

Prayer
When you call, help me to follow. Amen

Day 5

What not to wear on a total makeover: the power of body image

Trinny and Susannah advise me to layer my clothes. Daytime chat shows can revolutionize my life with a two-hour makeover of hair, fashion and make-up – although, in my case, I am sure it would take two *days*. More difficult is knowing what to eat. For example, to eat or not to eat carbohydrates, that seems to be the question. For those of us at the mercy of the fat police, it is difficult to find a consistent answer. There are some Jack Sprats who say eat no fat, while other high-profile experts extol the virtue of great English fry-ups, and the Atkins Diet has been followed by three million of us. Of course, that's before we even get close to mentioning different types of sugar, the South Beach diet and so on and so on.

Of course, for some of us, this is a matter of being healthy. For many of us, though, it is a matter of image. We long for the perfect appearance. One survey concluded that the 'perfect man' had George Clooney's hair, George Michael's teeth and Ewan McGregor's looks. The 'perfect woman' had, among others things, Calista Flockhart's hair and Imogen Stubbs' eyebrows. Most of us do not quite match these physical characteristics. Indeed, in such surveys, the body shapes of Vanessa Felz or Danny DeVito do not come out on top. So, we try – by means of many things from the rowing machine to fashion – to improve our image.

Sometimes, the pressure to improve our image is to do with our needing to be loved. A friend of mine had many problems with her self-image. Outwardly, she seemed confident and mature, but inwardly she was fearful of how others viewed her. She had an eating disorder that she carefully hid. If she did eat, she would make herself sick later. She cut herself on her arms and legs with knives as an attempt to cry out for help. She had to wear long baggy clothes that hid the scars and her thin body.

Then, her life began to change. It was not a sudden experience but a gradual journey to finding the love of God. There were special moments along the way when she felt this love, whether in floods of tears or leaps of joy. She saw that same love in Christians around her and she developed the courage to move on. It has been a slow process and it still continues. She has learnt strategies to deal with her eating disorder and God is healing her self-image.

In her home, she has a simple and profound poster. It shows a young black American, rebelling against inferiority feelings put on him by racists, proclaiming, 'I'm me and I'm good, cause God don't make junk'. Beside it is the picture of a human body, misshapen and in agony, nailed to a cross. It seems an odd image, but, for Christians throughout the world, it is the sign of a loving God who gives his life for all people – whatever the shape or colour of their bodies.

Bible reading
Luke 5.12–16

Something to think about
How does God view my body?

Prayer
Lord, thank you for the gift of this body and the opportunities in life it gives me. Lord, I am also conscious of the trouble this body causes me. Help me to be a wise steward of my body and to use it, the things I like about it and the things I don't like about it, for your glory. Amen

Day 6

Mr Data, *AI* and genes: what is a human being?

What is a human being? In the movie *AI: Artificial Intelligence*, Steven Spielberg uses the earlier story by Stanley Kubrick to explore what it means to be human. A young boy robot gains the capacity to love and be loved. Does this make him human? I found it a fascinating and disturbing movie. It left me with the question 'Is it the reality of love or even the reality of death that defines humanity?'

It is a theme that has been explored before. Mr Data in *Star Trek: The Next Generation* struggles with the same question alongside *The Terminator, I-Robot* and Kubrick's own supercomputer Hal in *2001: A Space Odyssey*. This rich vein of interest in Hollywood reflects questions that are part of our society generally. The growth of the power of computers has been rapid. Are we reaching the stage of having to ask our computers if you can turn them off? This is not just a fear of whether or not artificial intelligence will take over the world but also a genuine question: If computers begin to show intelligence or even self-consciousness, then what does that mean for human beings?

The developments in modern medicine also raise the question 'What does it mean to be human?' The ease of abortion and genetic engineering on human embryos creates controversy over when life begins. The pressure from some for legal euthanasia locates the question in the midst of suffering, disability and death. Even popular discussion of the possibilities of human cloning often concentrates on whether you would produce the same person.

Against this background, many people are ready to give an answer to the question 'What does it mean to be human?' There are those who stress the physical. Richard Dawkins, for example, speaks of humans as simply gene survival machines. Others go in the opposite direction and stress the spiritual. On this view, it is some eternal soul that makes us human. The mass suicide of 39 members of the Heaven's Gate cult in a mansion in San Diego in 1997 was based on the belief that a spaceship was hiding behind Comet Hale-Bopp, waiting to take their eternal souls to heaven.

In the end, Hollywood may be closer to the truth. It seems to me that the key to a good movie lies in the quality of the relationships portrayed. Indeed, it is our relationships that define us. My Christian faith holds that the key to being human is relationship – with both God and other human beings. I have found this a very helpful insight, one that gives me a foundation from which to consider the questions posed by the growth of technology. To be human is not a matter of intelligence, it is a matter of love.

Bible reading
Luke 5.17–28

Something to think about
How much do I value my relationships over other parts of my life?

Prayer
O Lord, I understand that to know you only as a philosopher; to have the most sublime and conscious speculations concerning your essence, your attributes and your providence; to be able to demonstrate your Being from all, or any of the works of nature: to discourse with the greatest elegancy and propriety of words of your existence or operations, will avail us nothing unless at the same time we know you experimentally, unless the heart perceives and knows you to be her supreme good, her only happiness!

Susannah Wesley (1669–1742)

Day 7

Is God into sport?

I love sport and can't get enough of it. When the Premier League season finishes, athletics and cricket are there to keep me going. Of course, I am an armchair participant, but it still dominates my life. Social and even church engagements have to be shaped around regular attendance at St James' Park to roar on my Newcastle heroes (and sometimes villains!).

Some of my religious friends are not too sure about this fanatical devotion. Some object to the large amounts of money involved in sport and argue that it could be put to better use. I have some sympathy with that. Others argue that the competitive nature of sport is unhelpful for our society. Still more feel uneasy, that somehow sport is trivial and unimportant to the religious life.

I believe, however, that God is into sport. At this point I am not going to make the old joke that Jesus loved rugby because he was good at conversions. Nor do I mean that prayer can be employed as a supersub when your team is 2–1 down.

It is much more fundamental than that. The Christian faith rejoices in the physical as it is a gift from God. Some Greek influences on early Christianity said that the body was evil and only the spiritual was good. While that view is still around today, it is not true to the Bible. God created this material universe and said that it was good. Indeed, the Christian claim that God became a human being in Jesus affirms our physical life, whether it be work, sex or sport. The apostle Paul opposed those who demonized the physical world by writing, 'Everything God created is good, and nothing is to be rejected if it is received with thanksgiving.'

That is why the link between sport and Christian faith has been so strong. You see it in the church origins of football teams, such as Aston Villa, and in the lives of sporting greats, such as Jonathan Edwards, Jason Robinson and Bernhard Langer.

Yet, at the same time, it is very easy for any gift from God to cause things to get out of perspective. When it ceases to be seen as a gift, it can easily become an idol or a substitute for God. Bill Shankly was famously asked whether he thought football was a matter of life and death, to which he replied it is much more important than that. If sport becomes too important, though, it loses something. Healthy competition turns into violence, the challenge of improving the body leads to drug abuse and the joy of sport is sacrificed at the altar of corporate money.

As a Christian, I want to enjoy sport, but remember, when all is said and done, it is just a game.

Bible reading
Luke 5.29 – 6.5

Something to think about
Am I enjoying the gift of physicality?

Prayer
Thou has given so much to me, give me one thing more, a
    grateful heart.
Not thankful when it pleases me, as if your blessings had
    spare days;
But such a heart whose very pulse may be thy praise.

George Herbert (1593–1633)

Day 8

Pearl Harbour: the real story

The trouble with visiting family during the holidays is, often, their limited number of TV channels and videos. Indeed, recently at my mother-in-law's, we had the choice of the joys of daytime terrestrial television or the one video she had, which was *Pearl Harbour*.

We opted for *Pearl Harbour* rather than feel guilty about our lack of commitment to the cash in our attic, moving to the country or finding out what we should not be wearing. It had been some time since I had first seen Michael Bay's movie, slaughtered at the time by the critics. Actually, it was not as bad as I remembered it to be – perhaps this time because I was watching it in the light of a story I had heard only a week before.

The previous week I was in the USA and found myself chatting to a man who had been at Pearl Harbour on that 'day of infamy'. He told me the story of Jacob DeShazer. DeShazer was a bombardier in the Doolittle raid, which daringly bombed Tokyo in 1942. Shot down during that raid, he was beaten, tortured and starved as a war criminal. 'My hatred for the enemy nearly drove me crazy,' he said. 'My thoughts turned toward what I had heard about Christianity changing hatred between human beings into real love.' He begged his captors to get him a Bible and, amazingly, they did. As he read the story of Jesus, he was captivated by how Jesus forgave those who crucified him. Asking for help from the risen Jesus, his life and attitudes were changed.

In 1948, DeShazer returned to Japan as a Methodist missionary. He also wrote a short book entitled *I Was a Prisoner of Japan*. One person who read this was an embittered Japanese ex-pilot, Captain Mitsuo Fuchida, who led the attack on Pearl Harbour. The message was completely different from anything the pilot had ever heard. All of his dreams had been shattered by Japan's defeat, but he found new hope in Jesus and became a Christian.

Remarkably, Fuchida, the Japanese pilot who bombed Pearl Harbour, and DeShazer, the Doolittle raider who bombed Tokyo, became close friends and spent the rest of their lives sharing the good news of Jesus as missionaries in Asia.

Ben Affleck, the hero figure, is centre stage in the movie, but DeShazer gives us a very different story about how lives can be changed and, indeed, how hatred can be changed into real love.

Bible reading
Luke 6.17–36

Something to think about
Whom do I need to forgive?

Prayer
O Lord Jesus, because, being surrounded with infirmities, we often sin and have to ask pardon, help us to forgive as we would be forgiven; neither mentioning old offences committed against us, nor dwelling upon them in thought, nor being influenced by them in heart; but loving our brother freely, as you freely loved us. For your name's sake. Amen

Christina Rossetti (1830–94)

Day 9

A hitchhiker's guide to the gospel

My childhood and teenage years were dominated by a stark contrast. Television was fun and church was boring. *Monty Python*, *Fawlty Towers* and *The Hitchhiker's Guide to the Galaxy* engaged my imagination and painted scenes that made me laugh out loud.

In *The Hitchhiker's Guide*, the late Douglas Adams pushed the surreal to the limit with improbability drive, Marvin the depressed robot and the restaurant at the end of the Universe. At school, we knew his proof for the non-existence of God off by heart. It goes like this. The Babel fish is a small object which, when inserted into the ear, allows you to understand any alien language. Now, it is so staggeringly useful that it must be proof for the non-existence of God. The argument is that God refuses to prove that he exists for that would deny faith. Hold on, says man, the Babel fish is a dead give-away, it proves that you exist and therefore you don't – QED. Oh dear, says God, I hadn't thought of that and promptly disappears in a puff of logic.

This of course, was another world to church. Stories in church were serious, predictable and all with a moral point. Sermons were humourless, apart from the odd cringe-worthy joke from *300 jokes to liven up a sermon*. The clever humour of the television that made you see the world differently was certainly not the world of Jesus – or so I thought.

That was until I heard a preacher who, instead of jumping off from a gospel story into a fine but unrelated moral lesson about kindness, stayed with the text. He pointed out that, when Jesus meets Nathanael for the first time, we find a routine worthy of Basil and Sybil Fawlty.

Nathanael, on hearing that Jesus comes from Nazareth responds with, 'Can anything good come from Nazareth?' Then Jesus joins in the irony. He says of Nathanael, 'Here is a true Israelite, in whom there is nothing false.' This is clever wordplay, although you will be excused for not immediately picking it up. You have to remember that 'Israel' is another name for 'Jacob' and Jacob is famous for stealing from Esau by lies and deception. The joke is therefore something like, 'Here is a child of deception in whom there is no deception.' No wonder Nathanael, who likes such humour, says to Jesus, 'How do you know me?'

The Jesus of the gospels often uses such humour to build relationships or convey serious points. We do him an injustice when we try to explain the phrase 'harder for a camel to go through an eye of a needle' by arguing that one of the gates of Jerusalem could have been referred to as the eye of the needle, rather than seeing the ludicrous picture of a camel trying to squeeze itself through an impossible opening and understanding the difficulties for rich people of getting into the kingdom.

A boring church cannot be allowed to make the Jesus of the gospels boring. Equally, in the humour of the world we need to hear a God who uses such humour to deepen our humanity and give us a different view of the world. Entertainment is not all 'trivial'.

Bible passage
Luke 6.37–49

Something to think about
In the passage above, look for the humorous pictures. How do they speak to your life?

Prayer

Thank you, Lord, for the gift of laughter, for the way it makes us feel, for the way it brings us together. Thank you for the creativity in entertainment and the way, through humour, you show us new things. Help me to use the gift of humour wisely. Forgive me when I use it to put other people down. Forgive me when I join in on jokes that degrade members of the opposite sex, or people with a different background. Help me to use laughter for your glory. Amen

Day 10

You gotta have faith

Richard Dawkins has made a name for himself as both an outstanding popularizer of science and aggressive opponent of religion. For Dawkins, 'religion is the root of all evil', acting as a virus among believers.

With his characteristic humility when he comes to theology, he says, 'Faith is the great cop-out, an excuse to evade the need to think and evaluate evidence.' He is reflecting that old kid's definition of faith as 'believing things we know aren't true'. It is as if Christians, when entering church, simply exchange their intellect for a hymn book.

Of course, Dawkins is right, but only for a small section of those who would call themselves Christian. The majority of Christians have a much more developed view of faith. After all, it is something that is at the centre of their lives and has been tested by costly decisions and difficult circumstances. I know a young couple, both with Ph.D.s, whose faith has led them to work as missionaries in China. I know also a leading lawyer whose faith has been tested by the death of a child.

These people do not take evidence lightly, nor do they live a schizophrenic existence between their professional and church lives. They understand that faith, in its biblical definition, is trust on the basis of evidence. Such faith is exercised in both religion and other things. Dawkins' science, in fact, involves trust on the basis of evidence. Scientists trust that the natural world is intelligible due to our experiments and theories. Further, in constructing a theory, scientists can never get an infinite amount of evidence *for* the theory and no evidence *against* it. There comes a point when they weigh the evidence for and against and are sufficiently convinced that they can trust to publish a paper or to send human beings to the moon.

Christian faith involves trust on the basis of evidence. The gospels offer us an amount of evidence for the life, death and resurrection of Jesus, such that we are convinced of his love for us. It is on that evidence that Jesus calls us to trust him and follow him as disciples. Now, of course, that evidence must be evaluated. There are some aspects of this universe that I find very difficult to reconcile with a loving God, such as the existence of natural evil and unjust suffering. This might be taken as evidence against God. However, the strength of the evidence I see in Jesus helps me to keep trusting God, whatever happens.

Of course, Christian faith goes further than simply trust in an intellectual theory. It speaks of trust in a person. Now, I can ask the question, 'Does my wife love me?' I can evaluate the evidence for and against, and that is important, but I get to the point when I need to act on the evidence. At some stage, I have to decide whether she does or she doesn't. If I decide that she does, I have to commit myself to her, trusting that my love will be reciprocated. Indeed, until I do that I will not fully experience her love.

Thus, Christian faith is not the great cop-out. It is the evaluation of evidence, followed by trust, which leads us into a living relationship with the risen Jesus.

Bible reading
Luke 7.1–17

Something to think about
What is my faith based on?

Prayer
Teach us, O God, not to torture ourselves, not to make martyrs of ourselves through stifling reflection; but rather teach us to breathe deeply in faith, through Jesus, our Lord.

Søren Kierkegaard (1813-55)

Day 11

Looking for Jesus in *The Da Vinci Code*

Dan Brown's bestseller *The Da Vinci Code* is now a movie, directed by Ron Howard and starring Tom Hanks. This ultimate page-turner is a pretty good story. A Harvard professor called Robert Langdon and Sophie Neveu, a cryptographer, work out that the secret of the Holy Grail is that Jesus married Mary Magdelene and that his bloodline continues today.

I am torn about this book. I enjoyed reading it and it entertained me on a dull train journey, but I teach theology at the University of Durham and it reminded me of a particularly bad first-year's essay. Some of the factual mistakes made me laugh, while others made me wince.

If this book was a work of fiction, then I would have no problem with it, but Brown claims at the beginning that there is a Priory of Sion and that artwork, architecture, documents and secret rituals are described accurately. It is that claim that changes things. In fact, there was no Priory of Sion, it was simply the result of a historical hoax. Second, he misrepresents, time after time, in the words of his characters, the history of the Christian faith, the Nag Hammadi texts and the Dead Sea Scrolls. Even undergraduates who have spent most of their first year in college pursuits away from their studies, these basic errors would be unforgivable.

Such mistakes are, of course, not new. In 1982, the same claims were made in the bestseller *Holy Blood, Holy Grail* by Michael Baigent. Why do such books sell so well? The Christian faith has been a powerful influence for a long time in western culture and anything that attacks such an institution is bound to be popular. Further, the figure of Jesus remains an engaging person, even in an increasingly secular society. In the contemporary search for who we are, Jesus seems to be someone to whom we return time after time.

I understand that entirely. As a teenager, I was fascinated by claims for ESP, UFOs and aliens. As a professional astrophysicist, I have examined science at its cutting edge in the origin of the universe. In exploring all of these, though, I have returned to Jesus to find out who I truly am.

Now, as a professional theologian, I know that the historical basis for the life, teaching, death and resurrection of Jesus is far more reliable than many of these other claims and considerably more so than *The Da Vinci Code* portrays. So, I watch Tom Hanks in the movie, with the knowledge that it is a story more like *Forrest Gump* rather than *Apollo 13*.

Bible passage
Luke 7.18–35

Something to think about
Can I help others to understand more the basis of Christian faith?

Prayer
Lord, give us weak eyes for things which are of no account and clear eyes for all your truth.

Søren Kierkegaard (1813–55)

Day 12

Marie Claire's hero

Among the many honours that David Beckham has collected, there is one for which he just had to stand still. Beckham is the first man to have appeared on the cover of the magazine *Marie Claire*. I found myself wondering what it is that makes Beckham so attractive to *Marie Claire*'s publishers and readers. Of course, in terms of looks, he has a lot more to offer than Peter Beardsley or even myself, as my wife was quick to point out. It seems to me, though, that his attractiveness is about more than that.

Beckham is attractive because he is both fit and committed. This football star is not only a sex-god (my wife's words), but also a committed husband and father. While the rumours of his playing away with Rebecca Loos were tabloid fodder for a time, he is still with Posh. Some may mock him, but, while everyone around him have often lost their heads, he has kept his. He inhabits a world of image and adulation, but shows the rarely seen quality of commitment, even after making mistakes.

This is the stuff of fairytale romance. In a post-Bridget Jones world, sexual attraction is good, but it is not enough. That excitement of romance must find its context in the commitment of intimacy. David Beckham combines the two. In this, I think, he is worthy of all the admiration he receives, because he points beyond the frustration and fragility of the one-night stand to what human relationships can be.

Perhaps there is even something more than this. Beckham is an example of someone who, in the language of religion, has experienced redemption. That is, his life has been turned around.

At the time of the 1998 World Cup, he was a hate figure, abused by the press and supporters alike after being sent off in the game against Argentina. There were many, including myself, who said that he should never play for England again after the stupid sending off. Beckham has caused us to eat our words. We were wrong and, four years later, even with panic over a metatarsal, he was captain of the England team. Here is someone whose life has been turned around, where the past no longer has a hold over the future. In the area of football, Beckham has worked hard, but he has also been helped, not least by his wife. The answer to the broader questions of human life – the major religions of this world, including my own Christian faith, believe – is that any life can be redeemed with the help of God.

Some readers of *Marie Claire* will no doubt long for David Beckham in purely a physical way. Others will see more. They will see their own hopes for romance and commitment in his story. They also might see their own hopes for their lives to be turned around. We all want to 'bend it like Beckham', but can we find someone to help us do it?

Bible reading
Luke 7.36–50

Something to think about
In which areas of your life would you like a new start?

Prayer
Lord Jesus, thank you that you are the God of new beginnings. Thank you that you are the one who comes to us and says, 'Your sins are forgiven.' Transform my life by the power of your love. Thank you that, with you, the past does not have a hold over the future. Help me to be honest with you and others for the mistakes and weaknesses of the past. Help me to own the responsibilities for my wrong actions and thoughts and the way they have hurt others. Help me, too, to trust in your power to give me a new start and, in response, I want to be committed to you. Amen

Day 13

Deep questions according to Hannah, aged four and a half

When my daughter, Hannah, was four years old, she turned to me in the car and said, 'Daddy, can we talk about deep things?' I smiled and inwardly congratulated myself on her intelligence and how that reflected well on her parents. Here was a child who outwardly appeared to be dominated by the triviality of Barbies, *The Tweenies* and a dislike of all meals apart from those shaped like dinosaurs and made of turkey. Yet, underneath, she wanted to engage with the big questions of life.

I felt proud. Obviously, with half of my life having been spent as a professional scientist exploring the origins of the universe and the other half as a preacher of the Christian gospel and teacher of theology, my influence was being felt by my daughter and, of course, I was the best person to answer her questions on such issues.

'What deep things do you want to talk about, Hannah?' I said. She paused and furrowed her brow. I waited with expectancy until she said, 'Swimming pools, they're deep ... and the ocean, that's deep ... and my bath, that can be quite deep ....' There then followed a good two minutes of her listing deep things before she became bored and went back to putting the legs of her Tinky Winky at quite painful angles.

I was put in my place. Yet, at other times, I have been put in my place by quite the opposite happening. I've expected the trivial and encountered the profound. Times such as when the taxi driver has switched off the meter to give us more time to discuss why people suffer, or when the woman in her late eighties who left school at eleven asks me if Stephen Hawking's theory of quantum gravity really makes a Creator God redundant.

People do need the space to ask the deep questions of life. The trivial and immediate things of life in our society and in the media are part of the fun of being human. It's just a pity that it often squeezes out the deep questions. Churches become places of petty squabbles and building funds rather than places of spiritual exploration. The media sees entertainment as its only form of communication. Even our education system at school or college often sees assessment and results as the only important parts of learning.

People do want to think and talk about deep things. I hope that, as my daughter grows up in our society, she will have enough opportunity to ask the deep questions. In my own excitement about the Christian faith, I have found it to be a context in which I can ask the deep questions, even if I don't always get answers to them. It seems to me that human beings need such a context if we are going to grow beyond the trivial.

Bible reading
Luke 8.1–18

Something to think about
Do I give enough time to discussing 'deep things' in my life, with those who live with me and in my church?

Prayer
Lord Jesus, I am sorry that there is so little time in my life for important things. I seem to spend my time rushing from one place to another, worried at how far behind I am, tired and often oblivious of the people around me. It's so much easier to switch on the television, music and the radio or to talk of trivial things than to come into your presence. Lord, I am sorry for how little time I give to nurturing the gift of your word. Give me a noble and good heart, to hear your word, retain it and produce fruit, both in my life and those of others. Amen

Day 14

The theme park experience: a life of thrills

The great thing about a theme park is that you can have a good lunch and go on a ride that allows you to see that lunch again! In Disney's Epcot Park in Orlando, I am told by one of the employees that, at the end of the day on the Mission Space ride, there is a competition between the attendants to see who has captured on their camera phone the most spectacular guest vomit.

It is an extreme ride – one of my favourites. Due to an ingenious system of graphics and very high-speed rotation, you experience some of the G-forces of a rocket launch and landing. It is certainly the closest I will ever get to space travel.

I love such thrill rides. Of course, there are moments – just before rollercoasters turn me upside down at 70 miles per hour – that I ask myself, 'Why I am doing this?' It is about experiencing things that are out of the ordinary and experiencing a little bit of risk.

Not only are thrill rides popular in our culture, but we have also seen a growth in extreme sports. While I might not fully understand why Matt Hoffman wants to jump out of aircraft on his BMX bike, I do understand why so many young people want to push the envelope of their existence.

As one sociologist said not so long ago, this generation is the most protected generation ever. Legislation has increased at an exponential rate to safeguard both children and adults. The typical baby shop now has as many safety devices as nappies. I am pleased that all of this has happened, but I do understand the human need to risk.

I believe that at the heart of the universe is a God who risks. The creation of human beings not as automatons, but with free will is an incredible risk. Yet, without free will and without a universe that both supports and challenges us, we would not grow and mature as people. Indeed, growth involves risk. While thrill rides fool my brain into thinking there is risk when in fact there is a carefully managed ride, *real* risk is about how I live my life in the web of relationships with other people and God.

Last summer, I was with 10,000 young people at a Christian event called Soul Survivor at the Bath and Wells Showground. They came together for a week's holiday and spent much of this time excited, screaming and experiencing awe-inspiring challenges. The centre of this event was not thrill rides or even the skate park – it was the challenge of Jesus to risk living life his way, at school, at university, in deprived parts of this country and throughout the world. In the commitment of many of those teenagers, I saw what risk is all about.

Bible reading
Luke 8.22–25

Something to think about
In Christian discipleship, am I too comfortable or safe? Do I need to risk more?

Prayer
Lord, help me trust you, the one who commands even the winds and the water. May my faith push me to take risks for the kingdom. Show me where I have become too dependent on my own resources and too safe. Amen

Day 15

I still haven't found what I'm looking for

Why does it always happen at birthdays? I am desperate to find a skipping-rope. Not just *any* skipping rope. This skipping-rope counts the number of skips and also times you as you skip. A birthday is fast approaching and I find myself searching the toy shops looking for this particular skipping-rope requested by my daughter, Hannah, aged 8 and 350 days. In fact as I drove from one toy shop to another, I couldn't help smiling as, on the radio, U2 sang, 'And I still haven't found what I'm looking for'!

At other times I am not smiling. In one toy shop, after searching all the shelves for some 20 minutes and concluding that skipping-ropes that flashed with lights were not appropriate, I saw one of those rare sights – a shop assistant. Moving forward quickly, I cornered her and asked if she knew whether her shop stocked my particular skipping-rope. She replied, 'If we have it, it will be in the toy section.' Quickly she moved off.

What I would have given for someone to help me – really help me. If I am honest, there are many situations in life where I need help and they are far more serious than my skipping-rope quest. How do I make sense of the world, cope with grief, resist temptation and find wholeness as a human being? The psalmist in the Hebrew Bible speaks very simply of 'the Lord' as 'my helper'. Thousands of years later, the baby born in Bethlehem is given the name Jesus, which means 'Saviour'. My Christian faith is unashamedly about a God who is a helper and saviour.

In fact, the same thing is said in that U2 song. It speaks of God who has broken the bonds and loosed the chains, even carrying the cross of my shame. Yet, concludes Bono, even with all of that, there is still the need to press forward. Life cannot stand still and faith draws us ahead to that time when we will see God face to face.

Christian faith doesn't claim to solve all your problems or enable you to know everything about everything – especially the location of a particular skipping-rope, but it is about a God who offers forgiveness and hope and releases you to explore and journey on. If only my shop assistant had pointed me in the right direction, then she would have been a great help.

Christian faith isn't the end of the journey, it is only the beginning. There is always something to the Christian life of pressing on to the higher calling of the Lord. The key is that the Lord himself is a companion on this journey. It is a journey of joint discovery that makes the searching joyful rather than frustrating.

Bible passage
Luke 8.26–56

Something to think about
How do I see God in my favourite music?

Prayer
> 'Tis Jesus the first and the last,
>> Whose Spirit shall guide us safe home;
> We'll praise him for all that is past,
>> And trust him for all that's to come.

Joseph Hart (1712–68)

Day 16

The wisdom of post-match interviews

I love post-match interviews with footballers, managers and pundits. The clichés and inappropriate images come thick and fast, from stating the obvious to the profound. I wait with baited breath for Big Ron to say, 'It's a game of two halves' and find myself wondering how, in Sir Bobby's words, Newcastle can engage in a dog-fight while rowing together in the boat.

Sometimes the comments are surprising, such as Stuart Pearce's, 'I can see the carrot at the end of the tunnel' or Barry Venison's, 'I always used to put my right boot on first and then obviously my right sock.' Sometimes we touch the sublime, with Paul Gascoigne's, 'I never make predictions, and I never will.'

Alan Shearer commented on his long-term future, having retired from Newcastle United, 'I've never wanted to leave Newcastle. I'm here for the rest of my life, and hopefully after that as well.' I know what he means. As a native of the North East myself, we have recently returned to God's own country. I find myself at St James' Park, standing with 52,000 others in adoring praise – at least, that is, until the match starts.

The images used in the Bible for life after death are not too far away from this. They are about going home to a place where you are loved and accepted. They are about being together in an exciting community, celebrating and praising the mighty acts of God, and, unlike St James' Park, the result is never in doubt.

In a pre-match interview with his disciples, Jesus talks about what happens after death. He likens it to a house with many rooms and speaks of going to prepare a place for them. Assuming that they recognize this as a reference to his death and resurrection, Jesus then says, 'And you know the way.'

Most of the disciples probably just nodded, having little idea as to what he meant. One of them, though, Thomas, is the equivalent of Five Live's Alan Green – that is, he likes to tell it as it is. Unable to contain himself, Thomas blurts out, 'But we don't know the way – what are you talking about, Jesus?' Jesus does not condemn him, but gives a sound-bite answer that has become a headline for Christians throughout the centuries. Jesus said, 'I am the way, and the truth, and the life. No one comes to the Father except through me' (John 14.6). It is an astonishing claim, which, as C.S. Lewis pointed out years later, gives us a choice: someone who said such a thing could only be one of three things – bad, mad or God.

I am convinced that the evidence points to God and this gives me hope of life after death. This is especially important, for the Christian life is the way of the cross. 'The way' for Jesus was one of suffering, rejection and death. The way that I am called to is to take up my cross daily. As a *Match of the Day* pundit might say, 'It's the toughest match of the season' with a glimmer of a twinkle in his eye because he saw the match earlier and knows the result.

Bible reading
Luke 9.18–27

Something to think about
What does it mean for me to follow the way of Jesus?

Prayer
Lord Jesus, thank you for the hope of that which is to come. Thank you that, through your life, death and resurrection, we can have an assurance of your love, forgiveness and new life with you now and after death. Help me to live in the light of that hope. Help me to follow your way. Amen

Day 17

The reality of *The Simpsons*

There are many things that bind our family together. Eating together is one thing and our shared love of Newcastle United is another. Our commitment to the Lord Jesus and participation in our local church is of central importance, but we have another strange ritual. That is, each weekday evening, we explore questions about what it means to be human. This does not happen around the dinner table, but it does happen around *The Simpsons*.

We love *The Simpsons*. Sharp, irreverent and insightful, it appeals to both my wife and I and our children. Its appeal has long been discussed, from the columns of TV reviews to academic theses, but I like it because of its reality –maybe a risky thing to say about yellow cartoon characters with three fingers who have worn the same clothes for the past decade. Most of the families I know who watch it identify the senior male with Homer and my own family is no exception as they make worrying comparisons between our physical and mental characteristics. That is, it is quite worrying until you remember alongside the liking for doughnuts and the television remote control, he is a man who loves his family and is attempting to survive in the midst of his limitations.

George Bush Senior, as he now needs to be known, famously suggested that he wanted American families to be more like *The Waltons* than *The Simpsons*. Yet, to this child who grew up watching *The Waltons*, the adventures of John Boy always spoke to me of a family separated from my experience, in terms of both time and values. We live in a different world from the slow-moving clichés of small-town America.

By contrast, *The Simpsons* live in a world that is familiar. I recognise the caricatures of Mr Burns, Principal

Skinner and Pattie and Selma as real people in my world. Like Homer, I struggle with laziness and selfishness, and yet value the importance of love. *The Simpsons* is outrageous fun, but it also speaks of the reality of forgiveness, faithfulness in marriage and family commitment.

It is also one of the few television shows that takes religion seriously. The Simpsons pray, go to church and explore the big questions of life with a reality that is lacking in so many other shows. Indeed, when God appears in *The Simpsons*, he is a lot of fun. He agrees with Homer's hatred of boring sermons and gives the Revd Lovejoy a canker sore – something that, at times, sitting in church pews, I would love to have done to certain preachers! There is also a subtle message about the reality of God. The convention among cartoonists is to draw unreal characters with three fingers to show that they are just creations, but when God appears in *The Simpsons*, he has four fingers. At the heart of *The Simpsons* there is reality.

Bible reading
Luke 9.46–50

Something to think about
What do I see of God in my favourite television programmes?

Prayer
Lord, as I watch television or listen to the radio, help me to hear your voice. What is good that I can enjoy, affirm and learn from? What perverts truth or dehumanises me and other people? What images, stories or words can be used to speak of you to others? Help me to be a full human and fully Christian consumer of the media. Amen

Day 18

The video games addict

There are good things and bad things about having a 12-year-old son. One of the good things is that I have an excellent excuse for making regular visits to shops with shelves of video games. The downside is that my son can beat me on any game of his or my choice. Despite this, I am still fascinated by such games. I remember my amazement in my childhood at the early table tennis game, with two paddles on the TV screen and a square ball pinging from one to the other.

Now, games take me into a different world. For example, *Halo 2* was one of the most eagerly awaited games of all time and took 1.5 million orders before it was even available. In fact, its release had all the hallmarks of the opening of a major movie. It has a fairly simple plot: supersoldier defends Earth from aliens with an impressive array of weapons and challenges. I tried being the supersoldier once and, by the time I had worked out how to fire my gun, the world had already been overrun and enslaved.

I can still dream of having another go and winning! Perhaps that is why video games are so popular. From the early days of defending Earth from the regimented swarms of descending space invaders, games have developed the sense of letting you play a significant part inside the story. Rather than simply watching 007 in the Christmas movie, I can become James Bond and save the free world. After shouting from the terraces, I can become the manager of my beloved Newcastle United and keep Alan Shearer from retiring.

There is something in all of us that wants to make a difference. I spoke recently to a girl who had been an angel in her school nativity play. After I complimented her on her performance, she complained that all she had to do was sit there and not do anything. In that way, perhaps, *Halo 2* is closer to Christian faith than wearing a halo as an angel in a school play. The Jesus born 2,000 years ago says that each person is special to God and has a key part to play in caring for the planet, building community and fighting evil in the world.

In his own Christian faith, J.R.R. Tolkien believed that strongly and told a story of how the small and weak hobbits were the saviours of Middle Earth. So, in my *Return of the King* game, I play the role of Aragorn, but know that I cannot succeed without Frodo. When I stop the game and switch the computer off, I find in my Christian faith the challenge and encouragement to make a difference to this world – and it is far more exciting than any game.

Bible passage
Luke 10.1–12

Something to think about
Do I believe that God can really use me?

Prayer
Lord, I often feel like a nobody – weak and helpless, irrelevant to the Church and the building of your kingdom. I feel that I have messed up, missed opportunities and I am not up to the standard of other Christians, who seem far more impressive and courageous. Forgive me. Show me the work to which you call me and help me to make a difference. Amen

Day 19

The force of *Star Wars*

Which is the best movie of all time? This is a really difficult question, for there both *The Empire Strikes Back* and *The Return of the Jedi* have their merits. As a *Star Wars* fan, no other movies come close – although both the original *Star Wars: A new hope* and the latest *Revenge of the Sith* would be runners-up.

The unfolding of the *Star Wars* saga has happened over my movie-going lifetime. The story gripped me as a 13 year old and has stayed with me ever since. Of course, there will always be those sad people dressed as Darth Vader standing somewhat self-consciously in the movie queue. Most people, however, including myself, simply looked forward to another part of the story of how Anakin Skywalker was going to turn into the evil man with the mask and severe asthma problem. This is the big question it asks: 'How is goodness seduced into becoming evil?'

As a Christian theologian, I was also interested to see the role of the force in this movie. Of course, some people have taken the force far too seriously. Sir Alec Guinness, who played Obi-Wan Kenobi in the first *Star Wars* movie, was once coming out of church when he was approached by a fan who said, 'May the force be with you.' Sir Alec, without thinking about it, replied, 'And also with you' – and then thought to himself, 'What a silly thing to say!'

George Lucas, the creator of *Star Wars*, would agree. The force was not put into *Star Wars* in order to create a new religion or philosophy on life. Indeed, when Francis Ford Coppola suggested that Lucas should make a religion out of *Star Wars*, Lucas laughingly refused. Lucas put the force into the *Star Wars* movies not to give an answer, but to ask a question. He said, 'I would hesitate to call the force God ... It's designed primarily to make young people think about mystery. Not to say, "Here's the answer". It's to say, "Think about this for a second. Is there a God? What does God look like? What does God sound like? What does God feel like? How do we relate to God?" '

In the midst of the special effects, merchandise and crazy female hairstyles, that question is central to *Star Wars*. Is there more to the universe than that which science can explain and technology can master? Lucas does not tell us what God is like, but he wants us to ask the question, which is something to take seriously – not just by those who want to make Jedi a religion, but also by so-called religious people who look down on popular culture.

The force enables the small, weak rebels to triumph over the technology of the Death Star. The belief that there is something beyond science and technology is the source of hope in *Star Wars*. However powerful the pull of the dark side, even for Lord Vader, in the end there is redemption.

This reflects, a little, Christian belief. Hope for the future for Christians is not built on our goodness or ability in science or technology. Hope is built on something beyond ourselves – God, who created this universe and, in the life, death and resurrection of Jesus of Nazareth, shows us that nothing in the universe can conquer life, love and goodness. It is on that basis of confidence that he invites me to join with him in the work of transforming this creation. It is this that always gives me new hope.

Bible reading
Luke 10.17–23

Something to think about
What do I see of God in the last five movies that I have seen?

Prayer

Hope beyond hope, you are our God,
We come before you for we have no other consolation.
Driven into darkness where there seems to be no light,
We recognize your hand shaping the slow tread of these
world-shattering events.
In you, Lord, we take refuge, let us never be put to
shame.

Hope of the silent tomb, you are our God.
We adore you for all you are in life's darkest hours;
You stand with us, when human words fail, and your
Word is all we can cling to.
We recognize your power even in absence and
desolation.
In you, Lord, we take refuge, let us never be put to
shame. Amen

Joyce Barrass, *Companion to the Revised Common Lectionary,*
Volume 4: All Age Worship, Year C, Epworth Press, 2000.

Day 20

The world according to soaps

What is it about soaps that is so addictive? It could be those tense moments of drama when out, of the shadows, Phil and Grant Mitchell emerge with a grunt of 'Hello Mum' to save Peggy. In fact, soaps have to exist on such storylines that build to a climax every 30 minutes. This 'exaggerated realism' of *EastEnders* means that there have been so many murders, divorces, weddings, fights and addictions that one wonders why the Queen Vic has not been turned into a community medical and police centre.

Is it the fun of characters that we recognize in ourselves or in others? Fred Elliott, Deidre Barlow and the Battersbys of *Coronation Street* may be extreme characters, but they combine fun with those aspects of human nature that fascinate and entertain us. Maybe it is the serious issues they raise, from teenage pregnancy to Alzheimer's, so vividly portrayed in the end of the life of Mike Baldwin.

Perhaps the real reason for my finding soaps so fascinating is that I can watch the joys and tears of other people's lives without having them living next to me. I want to see what happens to the Slaters, but it would be a nightmare to have them as my neighbours!

In that way, the soap world is very different from the real world, where I cannot be an anonymous observer. The lives of those with whom I work and live impact my life for good and bad. It would be lovely if this was all about 'Neighbours, everybody needs good neighbours, just a friendly wave each morning helps to make a better day'. Sometimes neighbours *don't* give me a friendly wave and sometimes they need my help in a costly way.

When Jesus spoke about neighbours, he told a story worthy of a soap opera. It features violence, hypocrisy and new relationships from different sides of the track. To translate it into a soap script, it would go something like this. Ian Beale is going down the road from Walford to negotiate a franchise for his quality fish and chips in the West End. However, passing through Piccadilly, he is set upon by the cast of *Hollyoaks*, down from Merseyside for a day trip. Lying in a back alley, he is seen by Revd Ashley Thomas of *Emmerdale*, who hurries on, conscious of his guest appearance on *Songs of Praise*. Some hours later, he is also seen by Liz McDonald, who cannot get her special dress dirty as she is picking up the annual Soap Awards for the most comebacks on *Coronation Street*. Then, Phil Mitchell walks by and sees his chance, not to finally get rid of his arch enemy but, rather, to pick him up, wipe away the blood, take him to *Holby City* A&E and then pay for him to stay in *Hotel Babylon* for the rest of the season.

The climax to the story as Jesus tells it is not something to make you watch again, it is a challenge to what this story means for your own life. The story of the Good Samaritan is not something simply to be enjoyed while eating supper – it is a direct challenge to taking responsibility for men and women throughout the world, all created in the image of God, regardless of their background. That is why the life of a disciple of Jesus goes beyond the omnibus edition of the stories of Jesus that is often known as Sunday worship.

Bible reading
Luke 10.25–37

Something to think about
Who is your neighbour where you live, where you work or among the people you have so far never met, either in this country or abroad?

Prayer
Lord, as I enjoy the world of stories and entertainment presented to me by the media, let me also hear your voice challenging me to be a Good Samaritan to those people and places where I can make a difference. Amen.

Day 21

Mobile phones: the next generation

I grew up in the 1960s, watching *Star Trek* and dreaming of being Captain Kirk. Indeed, as a five year old, I remember stealing my mother's powder compact, flicking the lid up and saying into it, 'Beam me up, Scotty.' Apart from covering the left side of my face with a coat of powder, it gave me one of those dreams that, in the future, everyone would have their own communicator.

I never imagined that, within 40 years, everyone would have mobile phones and that even the most imaginative ringtones would drive me crazy! Technology has developed at an amazing pace and the third generation of mobile phones give us picture and video options in a way that is beyond even Gene Roddenberry's dreams.

Yet Roddenberry also dreamed of a world where technology and science would lead to a new world order, where all people would be brought together. The trouble is that technological advances have not made this happen. While the Cold War may have ended, we still see wars between nations and injustice and suffering within nations.

Victor Hugo once commented on the French Revolution that revolution could change anything except the human heart. The root of our problems is not our lack of technology or education, but the selfishness, pride, greed and insecurity at the heart of human nature. Some may despair and paraphrase Scotty, 'You canna' change the laws of human nature, Captain!'

The religions of the world have never been so pessimistic. My own Christian faith is centred on the belief that an encounter with Jesus can lead to a dramatic change in terms of forgiveness of the past, moral strength for the present and hope for the future. Such a change is not achieved by myself alone, but happens in relationship with him.

We know the importance of relationships. Not even the most uncommunicative teenager is an island – a fact that mobile telephone advertising exploits. Human beings exist in and for relationships, with the need to communicate. Christian faith affirms this communal aspect of being human, but pushes it further. To fulfil what it really means to be human involves a relationship with the God who created me and loves me.

For this relationship, I don't need a third – or even fourth – generation mobile phone. I can communicate with God at any time and in any place. Whether on a train, in a shop or simply walking along, prayer does not require a monthly contract, nor does it bug other people with a shrill ringtone.

Bible reading
Luke 11.1–13

Something to think about
How can I pray more?

Prayer
Lord, teach me to pray. Amen

Day 22

The view from The Big One

In Blackpool there is one of the favourite places I share with my wife. It is one of the world's biggest roller-coasters, called 'The Big One'. It's not the most romantic of places, but we love roller-coasters and, when we lived in Liverpool, we would often drive up to Blackpool.

One day, we arrived and the town was very busy. There was so much traffic that we couldn't find a parking space. We drove around and around and around for ages. The atmosphere in the car became more and more frustrated, with accusations flying – 'Whose idea was this?' and 'You just missed a parking space back there!'

Eventually we found a parking space that seemed to be at least four miles away. We walked back into the centre – now not speaking to each other. We queued to go on the roller-coaster. On the ride, you are pulled up a steep incline to the top of the first massive drop. At the top, most people look down the big drop. However, let me tell you this. If you ever go to Blackpool and go on The Big One and get to the top of the first drop, instead of looking down, if you look over your shoulder, you will see so many parking spaces, you just won't believe it! Thousands and thousands of them. Once we see things from a different vantage point, the problem that seemed so great does not feel as bad.

Of course, I am not advocating going on a roller-coaster every time you become ill, get into money problems or go through the break-up of a relationship, but it seems to me that people cope with these things if they have another way of looking at them.

My own Christian faith often helps me in this. I used to think that faith would solve all of my problems and lead to me living a life that was as balanced and stable as a toddlers' roundabout ride. Now I know that it is not like that. Christian faith for me has been more like a roller-coaster, in terms of its ups and downs, its excitement and its challenges.

It also provides a different way of looking at the inevitable problems of life. Illness, bereavement and stress have been real but, seen in the context of eternity and a God who loves me, I have been better able to deal with them than if I did not have faith in these things. Faith gives me a different vantage point, reminding me that my life is not the most important thing in the world.

I will continue to love roller-coasters, for the excitement and the different way of looking at things that they give me. I will continue to love my faith for the same reasons.

Bible reading
Luke 12.22–34

Something to think about
What aspects of my life would change if I saw them from God's perspective?

Prayer
Lord Jesus, forgive me for my worry, my lack of faith, my fear and my desperate need to be in control of my life, my possessions and my heart. Thank you for giving us the kingdom. Help me to live today in the light of that. Amen

Day 23

Faith in spite of global warming

I'm sure that winters are getting colder. I asked my friend about this the other day. He replied that, in fact, they are getting warmer and the reason for them *feeling* colder is simply due to the fact that I am getting old. I could have argued the point with him but I would have lost. After all, he is the co-chair of the Scientific Assessment Group on the Intergovernmental Panel on Climate Change – in other words, he knows more about the weather than Michael Fish.

He has spent the last decade of his life working with the world's leading scientists, studying the effects of global warming. Whatever certain American Government officials try to say, the scientific community is united on this one – perhaps more than on any other scientific issue. Taking all the possible predictions of what will happen in the future, scientists agree that the global temperature of the Earth will increase in the next 100 years by between 1.5 and 6 degrees, due to the burning of fossil fuels such as coal and petroleum. The best possible case – of an increase of 1.5 degrees – doesn't sound too bad, at least for those of us who live in the frozen wastes of the north of England.

Remember, though, this is a *global* temperature rise. A rise of 1.5 degrees – never mind the worst possible case of 6 degrees – would lead to millions of environmental refugees as there would not only be those whose land would be submerged by rising sea levels, but also those whose crops and livelihoods would fail.

The scientific picture is clear, so why have we made such slow progress towards doing something about it? I asked my friend if he ever gets depressed at this, after having devoted so much of his life to it. 'No,' he replied and gave me three reasons.

The first is that he has seen scientists from many different cultures and countries working together on this. Second, he believes that the truth will eventually come to be acknowledged. Third, he is a Christian and believes that God still has faith in the physical world. This creation is not to be thrown out with the rubbish so that God can start again in heaven. A God who came to us as a human being in Jesus makes a statement that this world is important to him. So, as my friend comes to the end of his scientific career (and, of course, feels the cold much more than me), he has faith that there is hope for this world.

It would be good if a few key world leaders had the same faith.

Bible reading
Luke 12.54–59

Something to think about
What change in my lifestyle can I make today to care for the planet that God has given us?

Prayer
Change the world, O Lord, beginning with me.

A Chinese student

Day 24

Why do they get the weather wrong?

We decided to escape the unpredictable English weather a couple of summers ago and head for the sun of Florida. As it happened, we left London in the midst of a heatwave and found ourselves in the wettest August fortnight ever in Florida, with the added excitement of a tropical storm! By the time we returned to England, the sun had gone and the cold winds of late August were blowing across the North East!

Why isn't the English summer more predictable? Why can't science give us a detailed forecast for each day of the year in advance, allowing Wimbledon to be timetabled on sunny days? Is it because we don't understand the physics of the atmosphere or that the Met Office needs more powerful computers? In fact, neither of these is the problem.

The problem with detailed weather forecasting was discovered by a man called Ed Lorenz back in the 1960s. Lorenz discovered that the weather system was a chaotic one. That is, its laws *can* be known, but it is so sensitive that detailed predictions cannot be made. He characterized it with the phrase the 'butterfly effect', explaining that the weather system is so sensitive, the flapping of a butterfly's wing in Rio can lead to a hurricane in New York.

Such an effect is a reminder that the world is not as predictable as many think. Before chaos theory, some likened it to a clock – that is, a mechanism that is easy to predict. Of course, some systems in the universe are like this – for example, the movements of the planets that allow us to predict when a comet will pass close to the Earth. Many more systems in the world, however, are chaotic and we cannot easily predict their outcome.

The mechanistic view of the universe became very popular following the success of the theories of Isaac Newton. In philosophy, it was used to deny that human beings could have free will, as we were just part of the machine. In religion, it was used to say that God could not work miracles by poking his fingers into the predictable universe.

Today, scientists are much more cautious. We now see the universe as a much more dynamic and exciting place, where human freedom is real. Not everything is boring and predictable. Indeed, for those who believe in a God who created such a universe, they would expect to see him at work in not just the regularity of the world but also the unexpected and the surprising. In such a universe, science no longer rules out miracles.

There may even be hope of avoiding something that is very predictable about the English summer – a valiant Englishman's defeat at Wimbledon. We may just have to expand our expectations and root for a Scot!

Bible reading
Luke 13.1–17

Something to think about
Have I ever seen God work in an unusual or unexpected way?

Prayer
> Thank you, God, for your transforming love in the miracle of creation:
> The skipping calf and the cedar tree,
> The pulse of new life in the frozen ground
> Waiting beneath the rhythms of wind and weather.
> **Thank you, God, for your transforming love.**
> Thank you, God, for your transforming love in the miracle of Jesus:

He came humbly to the draughts and dusty rafters of
    obscurity,
In the corner of a stable, shrinking his radiance to the
    size of a candle,
To light up our faces and lives with wonder.
Thank you, God, for your transforming love.
Thank you, God, for your transforming love in the
    miracle of the Spirit:
The baptism that changes lives and destinies
Through the whisper of grace descending.
Thank you, God, for your transforming love.

Joyce Barrass, *Companion to the Revised Common Lectionary,
Volume 4: All Age Worship, Year C*, Epworth Press, 2000.

Day 25

Looking for the gospel in rock

When Ray Charles sang, 'I got a woman', not only did he produce an enduring anthem, he also exhibited a fundamental change in popular music. Charles, just like Elvis Presley, Little Richard, Jerry Lee Lewis and Buddy Holly, had grown up in a church shaped by gospel music. Gospel emerged from a combination of Celtic folk, English hymns and West African rhythms and had God at its centre.

Charles moved gospel into soul by replacing love of God with love of a woman. He said, 'I'd always thought that the blues and the spirituals were close musically and emotionally. I was happy to hook them up. I was determined to go all out and just be natural.'

Yet the relationship between gospel and rock and roll stayed close. Although Jerry Lee Lewis was expelled as a student from the Southwestern Bible Institute in Texas for playing a boogie-woogie version of the hymn 'My God is real' for morning assembly, the Beatles went off into Eastern mysticism and there are perennial claims about Satan-worshipping heavy rock bands, God is there in the background and, occasionally, right at the forefront. Indeed it would be difficult to understand the work of the Black Eyed Peas, Bob Dylan or U2 without reference to God.

The Greenbelt arts festival, held annually at Cheltenham racecourse, has, for the past three decades, been celebrating Christian rock music. This isn't a singalong with Sir Cliff or a happy-clappy praise party. Christian musicians and artists explore the complexities of the love of God and the call to be disciples of Jesus. While the words are more explicitly about God than general soul and rock songs, it shares its inheritance with them, all the way back to gospel. Its themes are recognizable, whether the listener is Christian or not. The search for love, healing and redemption intertwine with the need to be involved in a bigger story or concern and the joy of being in an uplifting communal experience.

Pop music can be trivial and a manufactured commercial enterprise. At the same time, Christian music can be navel-gazing and alienating. Yet, in the themes of protest and the hope for a better world, gospel, soul and rock share a power to shape human lives and touch deeper realities. That is why I will continue to enjoy gospel, rock and roll and pop even though I am getting to the age where I complain it is too loud and have to ask my children to translate the lyrics for me.

Bible reading
Luke 13.22–30

Something to think about
How do I see God in my favourite music?

Prayer
Lord, thank you for your creativity at the heart of beauty, music and art. Thank you for the gift of song and its ability to challenge us, inspire us and touch us with your presence. I pray for Christian artists and musicians, but also all who want to use music to strive for you and for a better world. May they use their gifts faithfully. Amen

Day 26

Desperate Housewives meet Alan Partridge

What lurks under the surface at Wisteria Lane? Avid viewers of the television blockbuster *Desperate Housewives* will probably reply, 'Quite a few more dead bodies buried just a few feet down if the past story is anything to go by.'

Yet under the surface of the television series about love, betrayal, friendship and seeking self-identity are actors whose lives are also about love, betrayal, friendship and seeking self-identity. If that isn't true of the viewers' lives also, a video game based on the series starts you off as an amnesiac seeking your own self-identity in a web of love, betrayal and friendship!

Desperate Housewives has seen a triumphant return to television for Terri Hatcher – once Superman's Lois Lane. Her memoir, *Burnt Toast*, tells the story of her unemployment, divorce, depression and loneliness. Television is fickle for all actors, especially female actors whose prized looks are at the mercy of both time and taste.

Television is, of course, exaggerated reality and there is this reality to all of our lives. We have our highs and lows in life, and at times are more popular than at others. Sometimes we are invited to the party, but then we can be forgotten, snubbed or our desperation to impress can be misunderstood.

There are times in life when things all fall into place. Work is good, family is great and our health could not be better. Then, at other times, relationships fall apart, we struggle at work, and even lose those whom we thought we would be with always.

Steve Coogan's comic creation, *Alan Partridge*, goes through such a collapse – losing his television show and becoming overly dependent on Toblerone chocolate. He is desperate to bounce back to his former popularity and also desperate to be loved. While most of us have not lost a television show, many of us understand the Toblerone.

It would be nice to think that, in this up-and-down existence, there is some security. For the characters – and, indeed, actors – in *Desperate Housewives*, it often appears that money gives you that kind of security. Yet, we all know that it is committed love that offers real security in a world that can change so quickly. Alan Partridge does not see the selfless commitment of his long-suffering PA, Lynn, but, without her, he would not survive.

It is in committed relationships of love and friendship that we have the freedom to explore who we really are. As a Christian, I look forward to seeking self-identity in the video game and I will continue to be fascinated by the complexities of Wisteria Lane. I also know, though, that I find in Jesus a God who is totally committed to loving me. With God I am always invited to the party, however popular, or not, I happen to be in life.

Bible reading
Luke 14.1–24

Something to think about
Where do I find my security in life?

Prayer
Meditate on the following words.

Go forth in peace, for you have followed the good road. Go forth without fear, for he who created you has made you holy, has always protected you, and loves you as a mother. Blessed be you, my God, for having created me.

Clare of Assisi (1194–1253)

Day 27

Bridget Jones: love on the edge of reason

I am afraid I don't get chick flicks – in terms of why they are so popular and, literally, as you'll never see me select one at the video shop. After all, they are all somewhat predictable. Girl looking for love meets Mr Right, who, although utterly gorgeous, seems to be Mr Wrong. Mr Wrong, who appears to be Mr Right, pushes the real Mr Right out of the picture. Mr Wrong stops appearing to be Mr Right and shows himself to be really Mr Wrong. Meanwhile, Mr Right stops being Mr Wrong and they live happily ever after – at least until the sequel. This predictable plot is made somewhat more complex by the changing emotions and feelings of the Girl, so supporting the common observation that men can never, ever, ever understand a woman's mind.

In contrast, look at the unpredictability of the genre of action adventure. Mr Right is wronged and then triumphs. Such subtlety, such tension, such uncertainty! Who said male intelligence was less than female intelligence?

Yet, I have to admit, chick flicks ask some fascinating questions and give us a deeper insight into what it means to be human. The character Bridget Jones' search for a good love relationship is not primarily triggered by the desperation of being alone at her mother's annual turkey buffet, but the sense that we find ourselves in such relationships. Julia Roberts' plea, 'After all ... I'm just a girl, standing in front of a boy, asking him to love her' in *Notting Hill* plays with concepts of what makes us special and how much we can forgive. The joy and romance of *Love Actually* interweaves a world of grief, betrayal and mindless sex with the question 'How deeply can we really understand this thing called love?'

When Jesus talks about the nature of God and his love, he often uses human stories to do this. God's love is so stupid and over the top, that he is like a shepherd who looks for a single lost sheep and forgets about the other 99 – a comic cameo part that would be well suited to Rowan Atkinson's Mr Bean. God seeking us is rather like a woman who loses a coin, turns the whole house upside down to find it and then is so pleased that she spends it on a party to celebrate the fact. Then there's that story about a father who actually shows what love is in the midst of betrayal.

If we are made in the image of God, perhaps the complexities of our relationships and the glimpses of real love we receive tell us something about God's relationship with us. 'Surely,' some might say, 'chick flicks are just about self-centred romantic obsession.' Of course some are but, often, romantic love becomes a much deeper kind of self-giving love. One of the most moving romantic movies sees Richard Gere give himself to death for Jodie Foster in *Sommersby* and, through the tears, you might just see in your mind the faint image of a cross from long ago.

Bible reading
Luke 15.1–31

Something to think about
Do I really know that I am loved by God?

Prayer

> Love divine, all loves excelling,
>   Joy of heaven, to earth come down,
> Fix in us thy humble dwelling,
>   All thy faithful mercies crown.
> Jesu, thou art all compassion,
>   Pure, unbounded love thou art;
> Visit us with thy salvation,
>   Enter every trembling heart.

Charles Wesley (1707-88)

Day 28

Celebrity love island of dreams

It was a choice between *Charlie and the Chocolate Factory* for the second time of the summer and Michael Bay's movie, *The Island*. While the youngest member of our family wanted Willie Wonka, the rest of us outvoted her.

The Island has some weaknesses, but, overall, it is an engaging movie. We meet Ewan McGregor and Scarlett Johannson in an enclosed world, dreaming of winning the lottery, which would enable them to go to the Island – the only part of the Earth still uncontaminated. However, soon, Lincoln Six Echo – McGregor's character – discovers that he is a simply a clone, grown for spare parts in case his 'sponsor' in the outside world is injured or becomes ill. The contaminated world is simply a myth to keep the clones in their enclosed world, and going to the Island is not the dream of freedom that they are told it is, but the nightmare of having your body parts harvested.

As we might expect from the director of *Armageddon*, the story is full of special effects and action sequences, but it does pose some fascinating questions. Some people will focus on the ethics of cloning human beings and how human clones might develop differently from the people they were cloned from.

However, I was struck by the point raised when Lincoln Six Echo is told what is really happening – that he is the product of consumerism in the extreme, a world where the rich, by harvesting from clones, can buy eternal life.

While the movie's tagline – 'They don't want you to know what you are' – might be understood to refer to the way the clones are misled by the myth-story of the Island, it could also be understood as referring to us. Just as the sponsors are exposed as using their wealth to extend their lives at the expense of other human beings, we live in a culture dominated by the myth that human life is fulfilled by power and money. While we build our security on weapons and wealth, we often dehumanize others in our world. As Make Poverty History and Live8 reminded us, the issues of fair trade, debt and the environment are issues of justice. We need to be careful not to exist in our consumerist cocoon, not seeing our responsibilities to other human beings.

The faith communities of the world have often taken a lead in reminding us of what it really means to be human. For example, Jesus taught that eternal life and human significance are not to be found in riches and power, but in our relationships with God and others.

Indeed, I seem to remember a similar point being made in *Charlie and the Chocolate Factory*, but I still prefer *The Island* and Scarlett Johannson to Johnny Depp.

Bible reading
Luke 16.10–31

Something to think about
'I shop therefore I am.' How true is that of me?

Prayer
Jesus, help me to simplify my life by learning what you want me to be and becoming that person. Amen

Thérèse of Lisieux (1873–97)

Day 29

Hello, celebrities OK in the heat of the spotlight?

While we seem to be fascinated with the celebrity weddings featured in the pages of *Hello!* magazine, we also seem to be fascinated with the endless tabloid tales of celebrity adultery, cheating, divorce and breakdown. Indeed, the breakdown of relationships – from Jude and Sienna to Brad and Jennifer – even to Arsene and Sir Alex – is compulsive reading.

Perhaps it is so fascinating because we know from our own experience just how fragile relationships can be. The careless word or the selfish act can suddenly sour what seemed to be a secure friendship or trusting romance. When such a relationship breaks down, it can sometimes never be regained. Some then see the need to justify their side of the story, either with friends or in print.

I find it interesting, therefore, that, along with many other religious teachers, Jesus stresses the importance of forgiveness over and over again. Some of his followers once tried to ask just how many times you should forgive before ending a relationship. Should it be seven times as some of the religious authorities said? 'No,' said Jesus, 'as many as 7 times 70 is what you should be looking for.'

Such an overwhelming picture of how many times we should forgive recognizes the reality of relationships – we are not perfect and we will make mistakes. It further recognizes how bitterness can eat away at a person in a situation where there has been no forgiveness. Yet there are two important qualifications. The first is where a situation goes beyond the realm of personal forgiveness. Christians are not called to continue to be victims in abusive relationships, but rather, rightly, should seek help in the form of separation and the law. Forgiveness operates within the context of the law. Thus, a church leader guilty of sexual abuse may seek forgiveness but must also suffer the consequences of such action.

The second qualification is that forgiveness of all sorts has a cost to it. To forgive is to take into ourselves the pain that the other person has caused. Supremely for Christians, this is shown in the cross. When Jesus was tortured and crucified as an innocent scapegoat, in the midst of his own agony and pain, he says to those who were responsible, 'Father forgive them, they do not know what they are doing.'

Some relationships may break down and we need to start again. Some may be saved by forgiveness, which is never easy but is powerful.

Bible reading
Luke 17.1–6

Something to think about
Is there a person whom I cannot forgive?

Prayer
Lord, you know the cost of forgiveness. Lord, you know that, on occasion, I can only forgive through your strength. Lord, you know that I need the help of your Spirit in this. Holy Spirit, come into my life afresh – give me courage, give me healing, give me opportunities to restore and forgive. Amen

Day 30

Ned Flanders

Surveys always seem to produce surprising results. One concluded that four million Americans claim that they have been abducted by aliens. This is surprising as it accounts for more Americans than can do long division! I find myself asking the question, 'Why would aliens want four million Americans?'

Another survey was even more surprising. People were asked who they thought was the most well-known Christian in the public arena. Neither Billy Graham nor even the Pope topped the poll. In fact, the most well-known Christian does not even exist. His name is Ned Flanders.

'Neddie', as his family affectionately call him, is the Simpson's next-door neighbour. He is a wonderful caricature of religion taken to the extreme, yet, for all his nerdy piety, he is a character who is presented with some sympathy. While Homer's beer gut pays tribute to the effect of overconsumption of Duff by someone in their thirties, Ned is fit and looks far younger than his age – 60. This he puts down to the three Cs – clean living, chewing thoroughly and a daily dose of vitamin church.

It is funny to make fun of Christians, but, whether it is Matt Groening in *The Simpsons* or Richard Curtis in *The Vicar of Dibley*, these writers often do so with a sense of respect.

Of course, some Christians are rightly mocked as they are more caricature than their fictional counterparts. From the scary TV evangelist to the self-righteous Christians who simply use the title proudly to mask their racism, hatred or guilty secrets, we see through the unreality very quickly. Yet there is more to religion than that. There are those, such as Mother Teresa in the streets of Calcutta, who receive the respect of all, even those who are not prepared to share what they believe.

Perhaps in all of this we see glimpses of respect for the life of faith in this increasingly secular society. While the Church, with all its divisions, outdated traditions and love of status, is a real turn-off for many people, the importance of the spiritual and a life that is centred on the values of Jesus, in terms of forgiveness and self-giving, still communicates to people.

In fact, yet another survey in Britain showed that 70 per cent of people claimed to have had some experience or sense of the spiritual. So I will continue to laugh at the caricature of Ned Flanders, but, in real Christians, we see the reality of faith and, on the whole, we like it.

Bible reading
Luke 18.9–14

Something to think about
Who are the Christians I admire the most? Why?

Prayer
Lord Jesus, we pray for our fellow Christians in the public spotlight of the media, whether they be in sport, politics or entertainment. Protect them and help them in the midst of temptation. Thank you for their witness and help them to embody the values and love of your kingdom. Amen

Day 31

Kids' *Mastermind*

Children make good television. Whether they are answering *Mastermind* questions and making the whole adult population feel inadequate or spelling words that the rest of us have nightmares about, the combination of innocence and sophistication is quite compelling. When it comes to asking questions, they show that same combination. Little Ant and Dec have a way of disarming celebrities and getting to the real person, whether it be Tony Blair or Kylie.

Children have the ability to ask questions that the rest of us are too embarrassed to ask. This is true not just in the area of entertainment but also in the area of faith. A book of children's prayers gives some examples. One child asks the very reasonable question, 'Dear God, did you mean for giraffes to look like that or was it just an accident?' Another, whose future is no doubt as Professor of Analytic Logic at Oxford, asks, 'Dear God, how did you know you were God?' Yet another asks, 'Dear God, instead of letting people die and having to make new ones, why don't you just keep the ones you've got now?'

I like these kinds of questions. Teaching Christian theology at university level, I often wish my students would ask these types of questions – questions of natural curiosity but also questions of security. You can only ask bold questions if you are sure of the relationship.

One of my favourite characters in the Bible is Thomas, one of Jesus' disciples. Thomas is great because he asks the types of questions that the rest of us want to ask but are too fearful to. Thomas just blunders in. He is the Jonathan Ross of his generation. As we saw earlier, Thomas is not satisfied with a cryptic 'And you know the way that I am going' from Jesus. It is only after Thomas asks Jesus what on earth he is talking about that Jesus replies, 'I am the way, the truth and the life.'

If Thomas hadn't asked the question, Christians would not have had one of the quotes that has become central to the Christian faith. In fact, Jesus always affirms Thomas' questions. In tradition, he has been called 'doubting Thomas', but that is unjust. I prefer to see him as 'Thomas the honest questioner'. His presence as one of Jesus' disciples and the way he is presented in the Bible says quite clearly that God is open to questions. Therefore, there has to be a place in churches where people like Thomas can ask such questions.

I find myself with many questions for God. When one of my brightest students, who had just started training to become a Methodist minister, was diagnosed with cancer and died within a year, I found myself asking the question 'God, why do you let this happen?' It is a question that I continue to ask. I don't have an answer, but it has been important to ask.

Faith does involve asking questions, though sometimes the answers can be very surprising.

Bible reading
Luke 18.15–17

Something to think about
Where can I ask honest questions of my faith?

Prayer
Father, I am seeking: I am hesitant and uncertain, but will you, O God, watch over each step of mine and guide me?

Augustine of Hippo (354–430)

Day 32

The curious case of Inspector Morse and Stephen Hawking

'What's the purpose of it all, Lewis?' asks my favourite Oxford chief inspector on the scene of yet another crime. The immediate context of the question is that there is a serial killer on the loose, but, with Morse, the question has a deeper meaning. Here is someone not only wanting to solve a crime but also ask questions of his place in a world that produces the glories of opera alongside the abhorrent sight of a mutilated corpse.

The question of purpose is not confined to Oxford. Scientists studying the origin of the universe have been asking the same kind of question. What is our place in the universe and why is it here? We are discovering a universe that seems to have a Goldilocks principle to it – that is, things have to be just right to allow carbon-based intelligent life to exist. For example, if the energy levels within the carbon atom were only two per cent different from what they are, there would be no carbon in the universe, which is quite important for us because we are made of the stuff. There are hundreds of such balances. They are so extraordinary that one of the world's leading cosmologists, Paul Davies, says, 'I cannot believe that our existence in this universe is a mere quirk of fate.' Davies, without any commitment to traditional religion, ascribes our existence to a cosmic designer, God.

Modern science has been extremely successful in explaining how the universe came into being via the Big Bang, but that does not answer all of the questions. Indeed, we might expect that, for, in everyday life, science does not explain everything either.

For example, a 'kiss' is 'the approach of two pairs of lips, the reciprocal transmission of carbon dioxide and microbes, and the juxtaposition of two orbicular muscles in a state of contraction'. Now that is a true scientific definition of a kiss, but if I were to go up my wife and say, 'Darling, I would love to get together with you for a reciprocal transmission of carbon dioxide and microbes', I know what the answer would be and which words she would use! Instead, therefore, in that context, I would speak to her about a kiss in terms of purpose and value and its demonstration of the love between us. Now, that is a very different description. Which one is a true definition of a kiss? They are different, but both are true. Indeed, you require both for a full understanding of a kiss.

So it is not surprising that even Cambridge scientist Stephen Hawking, in his bestseller *A Brief History of Time*, after 167 pages of description of how the universe came to be, says, on page 168, says, but that doesn't explain 'why'. If both Oxford and Cambridge are asking, 'What's the purpose of it all?' perhaps the rest of us need to take the question seriously.

Bible reading
Luke 18.18–30

Something to think about
What do I see of God in the universe that science discloses?

Prayer
Lord, forgive me for finding my purpose in life often in my money and possessions rather than you. Restore to me the wonder of both your creation and your salvation. Amen

Day 33

The desert of the real

'Welcome to the desert of the real,' says Morpheus to Neo in *The Matrix,* the hit movie of 1999. I love that movie and enjoy it more than the sequels that followed. It has achieved the unique status of teenage cult movie and being the subject of a philosophy module at Washington State University. It was one of a number of movies that explored 'virtual reality' – worried by the way that our experience of life is mediated by the television, internet and news organizations. From David Cronenberg's *eXistenZ* to Tom Cruise's character's difficulty of knowing whether he is dead in *Vanilla Sky,* there is the fundamental problem of knowing what is real. In addition, *The Truman Show* suggests that there is a 'real' life and an artificial one that we need explicitly to dismantle in order to see things as they really are.

The Matrix, written and directed by Andy and Larry Wachowski, tells the story of an office worker, Neo, who is helped to see that The Matrix is a collective virtual reality construction designed to subjugate his mind while his physical body is used as a battery to support the artificial intelligence machines that now rule the Earth. The Earth, far from the technological and safe world of the virtual reality, is, in fact, a desert ruled by robots.

It is a multilayered movie, with references to myth, philosophy and Christian theology. Along with the many allusions and subplots, central to the movie are two themes. First, the way that science can get out of control. Science and technology are ways in which we control the world, but *The Matrix* paints a picture of a fearful future where experiments in artificial intelligence have got out of control. Human beings, therefore, are being oppressed by their own inventions. Science has always had that capacity. The knowledge pioneered in Einstein's $E=mc^2$ led to the fear and tyranny of the Cold War nuclear arms race. The second theme is how we know the world as it really is? How much is our perception of the world true to reality? How do we know what reality is?

It is interesting that *The Matrix* sees the need for a messiah figure to keep technology in its place and show us things as they really are. Keanu Reeves as Neo becomes this figure – someone called to a special role with superhuman gifts. He is the One, destined to free other human beings from the mess that they are in.

This is an idea that I see as having been borrowed from the Christian faith. For 2,000 years, Christians have pointed to Jesus as the One, delivering us from the mess that we find ourselves in and showing us what is real. He, too, appeals to teenagers and some of the world's most distinguished thinkers. While *The Matrix* does not tell the story of Jesus, it does point to the need to look for a deeper reality to the universe.

In such a situation, I find Jesus both a challenge and a comfort. Time after time in his teaching, he claims truth and that this truth will set us free. In a complex and confusing world, I discern truth through those I trust and from experiencing it for myself. I find in Jesus someone I can trust and, although his view of the world is not always comforting, it is as real as it gets.

Bible reading
Luke 18.31–43

Something to think about
Do I hide behind any lies about myself or my world?

Prayer
Lord, I am blind and helpless, stupid and ignorant, cause me to hear, cause me to know; teach me to do, lead me. Amen

Henry Martyn (1781–1812)

Day 34

The problem of viruses

My wife had eight viruses last week. It took me two days to get rid of them for her, even though she should have been protected from them. Fortunately she was fine through all of this – it was her computer that was sick.

After emerging from two days of battle with Sasser worms and sdot viruses, I marched into the living room with that kind of male machismo which communicates 'job well done'. I shared with her my vast knowledge of how to avoid this in the future and how difficult, time-consuming and draining the cleansing process had been. I then went to my office and found that my own machine was suffering from its own case of winter flu. That's the thing with viruses. No matter how clever the anti-virus software is, there is always someone somewhere in the world who produces something even more cunning in its ability to infect.

Fighting viruses is an ongoing challenge, whether it be in the virtual world or the evolving biological world. In fact, it is not the only thing in the world which is like that. Superhero Mr Incredible, star of Pixar's *The Incredibles*, sums this up when he moans, 'No matter how many times you save the world, it always manages to get back into jeopardy again. I feel like the maid – I just cleaned up this mess, can't you keep it clean for just ten minutes!' I suspect he's not the only one. Even Inspector Barnaby must despair of the never-ending murders in Midsommer villages.

Christians understand this mess in the world as being due to a spiritual type of virus affecting human beings. It has traditionally been known as 'sin', although the word has been so corrupted today that many people think it simply refers to sexual misdemeanours. In fact, it is a way of describing that ongoing human condition where I am unable to do some of the things that I know are right and, at the same time, find myself drawn to things that I know demean me as a person and others around me.

Is there an anti-virus software that might help with such a spiritual problem? The Christian good news is the claim that there is. It is not to be found in a set of rules or instructions, but in a person. Experiencing the person of Jesus identifies sin, deals with its alienating effects and gives me hope to continue to combat it in the future. It doesn't remove the ongoing challenge, but gives me the resources to face that challenge. One day, I might hear the words 'job well done', but, until then, I keep on battling.

Bible reading
Luke 19.1–10

Something to think about
Are there areas of my life that need to be cleansed and changed?

Prayer
> Finish then thy new creation,
> Pure and spotless let us be;
> Let us see thy great salvation,
> Perfectly restored in thee;
> Changed from glory into glory,
> Till in heaven we take our place,
> Till we cast our crowns before thee,
> Lost in wonder, love, and praise!

Charles Wesley (1707–88)

Day 35

I'll be back

Arnold Schwarzenegger fulfilled his promise to 'be back' in *Terminator 3: Rise of the Machines*. Some have said, unkindly, that playing a cyborg killing machine is the role that best suits his acting abilities, but it is certainly the role for which he is most famous. *Terminator 3* continues the story and Schwarzenegger's earlier terminator again defends the rebel leader John Connor against the most sophisticated cyborg killing machine yet – an indestructible female who is able to change shape and disappear altogether.

James Cameron's original *Terminator* movies not only made 'I'll be back' the impression that most of us have done really badly in recent decades but also introduced a pessimistic vision of the future where war decimates millions and machines attempt to take over the world.

Yet, alongside *Terminator 3*, we have Schwarzenegger becoming the Governor of California. As one commentator has put it cynically, another of Schwarzenegger's movies sums up politicians – *True Lies*.

It is an interesting contrast – the Uzi machine-gun and the ballot box. Both have had their advocates in terms of changing society and giving hope for the future. With the present widespread public cynicism concerning politicians, force may seem to be the more effective option.

The trouble is, however exciting violence might be, inevitably it leads to sequels. As the people of Northern Ireland, the Middle East and Iraq know only too well, the way of violence tends to breed more violence and never leads to a lasting peace.

That's why I want to keep faith with politics, despite all the associated difficulties of spin and media-dominated elections. The world does face an uncertain future, with the rate of technological advance bringing many challenges in the areas of artificial intelligence, genetic engineering and fair distribution of wealth. Terrorism and war are never far away.

Jesus once told a story about a landowner who gave responsibility to his servants and said that, some time in the future, 'I'll be back.' When he returned, the servants were judged on how they had used the gift of responsibility. So, said Jesus, use your God-given responsibility in this world wisely, for one day you will be called to account.

Bible reading
Luke 19.11–27

Something to think about
Am I participating enough in political debate about our society and the world?

Prayer
    Creator God, we pray
    for the coming of your kingdom upon earth:
    for the righting of wrongs;
    for the freeing of the oppressed;
    for the ending of wars;
    for the peaceful resolution of conflict;
    for the banishment of poverty and hunger.
    Your kingdom come: your will be done.

    Saviour God, we pray
    for a new age for humankind:
    for the righting of distorted values;
    for the freeing of those imprisoned by guilt, fear or
        despair

for the ending of hatred and intolerance;
for peaceful relationships of respect and
    understanding;
for the banishment of inhumanity and indifference.
Your kingdom come: your will be done.

Spirit of God, we pray
for the renewal of the church;
for the righting of past betrayals;
for the freeing of those too afraid to love;
for the ending of division;
for the peaceful resolution of disagreements;
for the banishment of complacency and shallow
    faith.
Your kingdom come: your will be done.

Christine Odell, *Companion to the Revised Common Lectionary,
Volume 1: Intercessions*, Epworth Press, 1998.

Day 36

Fame – I'm going to live ... for at least 15 minutes

Everyone wants their 15 minutes of fame, but Andy Warhol when he coined that phrase did not expect the explosion of reality and interactive television that would allow so many people to dream about living the dream.

Popstars, Pop Idol, Fame Academy and *The X Factor* have been part of a phenomenally successful TV genre that has launched the careers of Will Young and Liberty X, but do you still remember David Sneddon and Gareth Gates? *Big Brother* has given us Brian Dowling and Jade Goody, as well as the non-celebrity Chantelle who, because she looked like celebrity Paris Hilton, became a celebrity thanks to *Celebrity Big Brother*. These programmes pick up on our longing for fame, as if when we find it we will be able to sing, 'I'm gonna live forever, I'm gonna learn how to fly'!

For those of us who never will experience our own 15 minutes of fame, we are fascinated with those who pursue it and then have to cope with the reality. The half a million copies of *Hello!*, *OK* and *Heat* magazines sold weekly are full of the joys and, indeed, the sorrows of fame.

Fame offers a lot in our culture – money, status, sex, respect and power – yet it doesn't meet every need. The tabloids parade the misery experienced by celebrities as well as their fun. For it seems to me that the heart of being human is not to be found in the amount of money or number of sexual partners that I can amass, or even in whether or not my name will live on forever. The heart of being human is love.

That's why, for all the novelty songs about 'Cheeky girls', popular culture keeps returning to the longing to be loved and the search for that secure relationship where you can be yourself. Robbie Williams, with candid honesty in his songs and interviews, makes that point over and over again.

The world has always been like that. Two thousand years ago, a man was welcomed into Jerusalem riding on the back of a donkey while the crowds waved palm branches and exclaimed, 'Hosanna'. Yet, within a week, his celebrity status was being mocked as he died, nailed to a cross of wood. The Christian Church remembers this, especially in the days we call Holy Week. It remembers especially his death as being an act of God's love for every human being, whether they are powerful or powerless.

As someone who has never been famous, I sometimes dream of what it would be like. I am more thankful, though, for the secure relationships with friends and family and knowing that there is a God who loves me. In this way, I do not have to fear the nightmare of my life, gifts and worth being summed up in the comments of Simon Cowell and Sharon Osborne.

Bible reading
Luke 19.29–44

Something to think about
If I had 15 minutes of fame, what would I use it for?

Prayer
>   When I survey the wondrous cross,
>   On which the Prince of Glory died,
>   My richest gain I count but loss,
>   And pour contempt on all my pride.

Isaac Watts (1674–1748)

Day 37

The future according to George W. Bush

I love 'The collected wit and wisdom of George Bush'. While I might have difficulty with some of his policies, I do love the way he says it.

President Bush, along with many other public figures having to give a number of public speeches and interviews, has been prone to the occasional puzzling pronouncement, especially about the future. Let me give you a few examples. 'I believe we are on an irreversible trend toward more freedom and democracy – but that could change' is a classic.

Then, 'One word sums up probably the responsibility of any Governor, and that one word is "to be prepared".' 'If we don't succeed, we run the risk of failure' needs to be pondered.

Finally, the President's comment that 'The future will be better tomorrow' unwittingly sums up what many of us hope to be the case.

We would like the future to be better tomorrow because, from the standpoint of today, it does not look all that hopeful. A hundred years ago there was great faith in the future. The dream of human progress was that we were on an irreversible trend towards a new, perfect society. Science, technology and education would be the engines of such progress and their success was assured.

Such a dream was embodied in Gene Roddenberry's *Star Trek*. Science, in the context of space exploration, allowed Captain Kirk to boldly go where humans had never been before – that is, a perfect human society where the only major problem was the occasional Klingon.

The trouble is that the dream of human progress has turned into a nightmare. Science and technology have allowed us to land on the moon, but have also been used to construct the gas chambers of Auschwitz and pollute the planet with greenhouse gases.

Science is fantastic in what it can achieve, but it cannot deliver justice or, indeed, solve the problems of a greedy world that destroys the environment. A missile defence shield, greater airport security or attacking countries seen to be a potential threat will not, by themselves, assure us of peace or give people hope.

The Christian faith, which President Bush follows, does not base its hope solely on human beings. It points to a God who is both judge and deliverer – giving science and technology a moral dimension and the world hope based on something more than our easily corrupted abilities. To be prepared for the future is not to put our faith in science or in technological power. Nor is it to believe that a nation's security and stature are to be found in its military power. It is, in the words of President Bush's own American Declaration of Independence, to be a 'nation under God'.

Bible reading
Luke 20.1-19

Something to think about
Where did Jesus' authority and confidence for the future come from?

Prayer
Lord, we pray for those in government, at local, national and international levels. Give to them your guidance and help them to serve with integrity, justice and compassion. We pray especially for Christians who hold public office and ask that you would use them to build your kingdom. May they be sources of hope and witnesses to your justice and saving work. Amen

Day 38

Googling myself

The other day I tried to find myself on the internet. I felt rather guilty about doing such a thing and was worried that someone might walk in and find me trying to find myself.

The words 'David Wilkinson' brought an amazing 162,000 hits. I was overwhelmed at how important I seemed to be. That feeling was somewhat short-lived, however, as I began to realize that I was lost in a sea of David Wilkinsons. David Wilkinson the novelist, not me. David Wilkinson, the designer of the screw-cutting lathe in 1794, not me. Then there was David Wilkinson the rugby player, the software designer, the masters student in robotics, the dentist, the general manager of The Dorchester, the designer of virtual internet gravestones, and even the David Wilkinson who had created his own web site because he was a disgruntled customer of his local car firm. The first few pages of hits seemed oblivious to my meagre achievements or even to my existence.

It was an important lesson in humility. A former president of the USA – long before the internet had been invented – used to go through an evening ritual to limit his pride. He would look up at the night sky and identify the Andromeda galaxy in the great square of Pegasus. He would then say, 'That galaxy has 100 billion stars, each as large as our own Sun. It is one of 100 billion galaxies in the universe, each as large as our own Milky Way.' Then he would pause for a moment and say, 'Now I feel small enough, I can go to bed.'

The trouble with feeling so small is that it is easy to feel totally insignificant. In our ever-expanding knowledge of the universe and increasing technological world, we are faced with the question 'Do I matter?' A university department increasing in its student numbers was worried that some students might feel unsupported. They decided to contact each student with a letter of support. Unfortunately, someone pressed the wrong button on the computer and each student received a letter that began, 'Dear Student Number 20348, We have a personal interest in you'.

Human significance is given not by statistics or achievements or power, but by relationship. The love of my wife and children make me feel special and unique, whatever the internet says. My Christian faith, too, which says that I am loved personally by God, has helped me to see myself as more than a speck of dust in a vast universe.

In the light of that, perhaps I need to spend more time investing in relationships, for it is in relationship that I find myself, rather than on the internet.

Bible reading
Luke 20.41–21.4

Something to think about
Am I giving enough time to friends and family?

Prayer
For a short period of time, think about those members of your family or friends who are close to you. Pray for each one, thanking God for them, confessing any times you have failed them or hurt them and asking for healing of relationships. Ask God now to show you how you can serve them and love them. Ask for God's presence and power to be at work in their lives.

Day 39

Armageddon without Bruce Willis: things can only get worse

'Things can only get better' were the words sung to celebrate New Labour's election victory when they first took power. Their political opponents will quickly say that is still the case many years on.

In contrast to this song, science in the past few years has been singing, 'Things can only get worse – much worse.' In fact, Private Frazer's words in *Dad's Army* wouldn't be out of place – 'We're doomed.'

First, the bad news. The Earth can be hit, potentially, by one of 2,000 asteroids, the orbits of which intersect with ours, not to mention quite a few wandering comets. The impact of one of these objects would be the equivalent of two million Hiroshima-sized nuclear bombs. This kind of event, some 65 million years ago, may be the reason for the extinction of the dinosaurs. Of course, Bruce Willis would be able to save us from such an Armageddon – that is, if we saw the asteroid soon enough, were able to assemble the space technology to do something about it and afford his contract.

Second, the even worse news. In the last couple of years, scientists have found that the universe is expanding at an ever-increasing rate. Nobody quite expected this and we still don't understand what is causing it. However, we do know what it means for the universe. The beauty of the stars at night will be replaced by cold darkness as the stars switch off and the universe becomes too chilly for life, including ours, to exist. This future is inevitable and there is nothing that we humans – including politicians – can do about it.

Now, this will only happen in 20 billion years, so, as you were! You might say, 'Well, is it worth worrying about, then?' In the movie *Annie Hall,* the young Woody Allen is so worried about the expansion of the universe that he cannot do his homework. 'Some day it will break apart,' he tells his shrink, 'and that will be the end of everything.' 'But,' his mother replies, 'You're here in Brooklyn! *Brooklyn* is not expanding!'

The trouble is, the end of a story often affects how you view the rest of it. If Miss Marple wasn't able to solve the crime and simply said, 'This is futile! I'm going back to St Mary Mead and I'll never be nosey again', we would feel cheated at the end of the book.

Some scientists feel the same way about the end of the universe. One says, 'The more the universe seems comprehensible, the more the universe seems pointless.' This has led some scientists to ask if there is anything beyond the universe that can save us from such despair and give hope. In fact, it has led them not to Bruce Willis, but to God.

Bible reading
Luke 21.5–38

Something to think about
How does my belief about the future change the way that I live today?

Prayer
O Lord, let us not live to be useless,
for Christ's sake. Amen

John Wesley (1703–91)

Day 40

Delia, Jamie and food, glorious food

Is it just me or have we gone cooking mad? As a child, fish fingers and chips seemed to take forever to prepare and became quite exotic if a tin of peas was added. Now, people buy recipe books and actually use them. *Ready, Steady, Cook* shows you what you can do in 20 minutes with an idiosyncratic bag of groceries, as long as you have an experienced chef in your kitchen and have remembered also to buy cream, butter, herbs, spices, top-quality knives and a full assortment of the latest kitchen gadgets. Jamie Oliver crusades against poor-quality school meals and Delia shows me the *right* way to boil an egg.

I am also surrounded by adverts encouraging me to buy new types of sauces, puddings, pizzas and crisps, while also being told that I need to cut down and eat more healthily. Eating disorders abound while, at the same time, so much of the world is literally starving.

There is something very important about food that goes beyond it simply providing our bodies with fuel. Food becomes a focus for community, combining hospitality with the opportunity to create significant moments for sharing lives. The family eating together and talking over their days, the romantic meal – one person asking another out for the first time – and the dinner party where friends can relax, joke and share serious concerns – at moments like these, you feel a sense of togetherness.

That is why it is a scandal that we live in a world where there are those who do not have enough to eat. It is not just a matter of sharing the world's resources, but also of people being alienated from true human community.

It is significant that, the night before he died, Jesus ate a meal with his disciples. It summed up the hospitality of his love and acceptance of them. It reminded them of the friendship they shared and the new community they were being called to be. It was also one of those significant moments when Jesus interpreted the meaning of his death and how they should relate to one another.

This meal was also a Passover meal, specially prepared, and the different foods had symbolic significance – the salt water represented the tears that the slaves in Egypt had cried, and the Passover lamb represented God's deliverance. In a similar way, Christians have always seen the importance of eating together – indeed, making it central to worship. The sharing of bread and wine is about Jesus inviting us to his table as friends, recognizing the reality of our community life together and remembering, in the bread and wine, both God's sacrifice for us and the assurance of a future heavenly banquet.

At a time when we were struggling as a family, with ill parents, overwork and young children, a woman baked us a cake. As my wife ate her piece, she described it as tasting of heaven. It was an old recipe of community, solidarity and Christian love and it demonstrated to us the risen presence of Jesus in the world.

Bible reading
Luke 22.7–23

Something to think about
Are there ways that my offering Christian hospitality can help build the kingdom?

Prayer
Lord Jesus, in the midst of your preparation for the cross, you broke bread with your friends. In the midst of the pressures and temptations in my life, help me to make space to share with you and others. Amen

Day 41

'What happens at the end of *Titanic?*'

I have a friend who is as off the wall as Phoebe in *Friends*. She once went to see the movie *Titanic* and, when I asked her what she thought of it, she replied, 'I was so disappointed, I expected a happy ending!'

I love stories with happy endings. I want Dot Cotton to live happily ever after in *EastEnders*, for James Bond to get out of the situation of certain death, confound the crazy and somewhat overacted villain and his country, yet again. Yet, if I am honest, I know that these created words are deficient. They do not do justice to the reality of life, where my friends are not healed of cancer and politically complex situations are not resolved simply.

Nor do they do justice to the significance of death. Some of the most moving moments in movies are to be found in the sacrifice of one human being for others. I have already mentioned Bruce Wills. His character stayed behind to blow up the asteroid in *Armageddon*. Others are Richard Gere's character maintaining his love for Jodie Foster in *Somersby* or the self-sacrifice of Gandalf in *The Fellowship of the Ring*. These are all deaths that have significance. When Sir Alec Guinness read the script of the first *Star Wars* movie and saw that Obi-Wan Kenobi would die halfway through the movie, he almost pulled out. Yet that moment when Obi-Wan sacrifices his own life so that Luke and the rebels can escape the Death Star becomes one of the defining moments of *Star Wars*.

Happy endings are not everything, then. The day of Good Friday is a day of celebration for Christians. It may sound odd to celebrate the horrific death by crucifixion of one of the world's most respected and influential people, but it is the significance of the death of Jesus that

Christians celebrate. I don't fully understand that significance, but I do see a number of important things.

First, I see God becoming a human being in Jesus and entering the reality of my world – a world of death and unjust suffering. Then I see God, in Jesus, showing his love for me by giving himself up to death. Finally, I see God, in Jesus, having died to offer me forgiveness and a new start for the future. He is not a God who is merely a spectator. He is a God who gets involved – so seriously that he experiences death. That's why the cross is so important for Christians.

The death of Jesus is not a happy ending in Hollywood movie terms, but there is something more important about it than that. Its achievement means that this day can be called 'Good Friday'. Remember, the sequel is in three days' time.

Bible reading
Luke 23.32–56

Something to think about
What does the death of Jesus mean to me?

Prayer
Jesus, you died for me and I am loved. Thank you. Amen

Day 42

The purpose of life?

A couple of years ago, a national newspaper invited people to write in to answer the question, 'What is the purpose of life?' One person followed the Richard Dawkins view, that human life is simply a gene survival mechanism – a means of passing the genes down to the next generation. I have to say, that didn't excite me a great deal. A football fan wrote in and said, 'The purpose of life is Newcastle 2, Sunderland nil.' Now, as a Newcastle fan myself, I could see his point! However, my mind was drawn to the person who simply wrote, 'The purpose of life is death.' Profound but not very encouraging on a wet Monday morning over the cornflakes.

I couldn't help remembering the other day when I attended a lecture given by an eminent philosopher. He was talking about the meaning and purpose of life as he saw it and as great thinkers down the centuries have discussed it. At the end of the extremely eloquent and stimulating lecture, a young student asked, 'But what happens at death?' 'I don't know, I've never died', was his response. It was a clever response and most of us laughed. Not the girl who asked the question, however. She pushed him again, 'But how can we understand life if we cannot understand death?' Good point, I thought. This time he replied, 'The only way we would ever know is if someone died and then came back to life to tell us.'

Suddenly, I saw the extraordinary power of the claim of the Christian faith. What is the meaning of life, if death is the end? How do we know if death is the end? The Christian claim is that death is *not* the end and the evidence for that is the resurrection of Jesus of Nazareth.

That resonated with my life as an astrophysicist – studying stars, galaxies and the Big Bang – during which time I saw that science could answer many questions, but not all of them. As Stephen Hawking says in *A Brief History of Time*, we are still left with the question 'Why?' The resurrection of Jesus gives me evidence for a deeper purpose in the universe and my human life.

This is the time of the year when Christians celebrate that resurrection. It gives hope for life after death and, indeed, hope for the future of the world. This life is not all there is. Indeed, with the resurrection comes a bigger perspective on things. We are more than gene survival machines. Human beings are more significant than our victories or defeats in this life. While this life may lead to death, that's not the end of the story.

Bible reading
Luke 24.1–12

Something to think about
Does the resurrection change my perspective on life?

Prayer
Alleluia, Christ is risen! He is risen indeed, Alleluia!
Alleluia, Christ is risen! He is risen indeed, Alleluia!
Alleluia, Christ is risen! He is risen indeed, Alleluia!
Alleluia, Christ is risen! He is risen indeed, Alleluia!

Risen Lord, we celebrate your victory over sin, death and evil. Help me to see the whole world from this perspective. Help me to face sin, death and evil with confidence in you, and work with you to redeem all people and all things. Amen